WRITING
A Practical Guide for
Business and Industry

WRITING
A Practical Guide for Business and Industry

CHARLES W. RYAN

John Wiley & Sons, Inc.
New York • London • Sydney • Toronto

Editors: Judy Wilson and Irene Brownstone
Production Manager: Ken Burke
Editorial Supervisor: Winn Kalmon
Composition and Make-up: Winn Kalmon

Library of Congress Cataloging in Publication Data

Ryan, Charles William, 1929–
  Writing: a practical guide for business and industry.

  (A Wiley self-teaching guide)
  1. Commercial correspondence--Programmed
instruction. I. Title.
HF5726.R93   651.7'5'077   74-4289
ISBN 0-471-74789-0

Printed in the United States of America

74   75   10 9 8 7 6 5 4 3 2 1

For Elaina and the little one.

To The Reader

If you are a technical professional such as an engineer, a systems analyst, a physicist, or a chemist, if you hold a management position in industry, business, or government, if you are a technician, if you are employed as a writer in business or industry—in short, if your work requires you to write anything beyond an occasional letter, this book is for you. Writing: A Practical Guide for Business and Industry focuses on how to write and produce basic documents, from research and progress reports, proposals, and specifications all the way to brochures and manuals. This broad area we call technical writing. (The term technical writer here will refer not only to the person whose major job is writing, but to anyone who writes on technical subjects.)

You must understand first of all that there is writing and there is technical writing. They are not the same thing. All writing is communication of one kind or another. The many kinds of writing are distinguished from each other in ways that are sometimes obvious, sometimes subtle. Style, content, and approach differ, but the main difference lies in what is communicated; that is, the essential purpose of the writing.

All of Shakespeare is literature. A novel by Somerset Maugham or F. Scott Fitzgerald is literature. Many people would say that a Harold Robbins novel is not literature. But Robbins has made a pile of money with his books because he knows the purpose of his writing and he does it very well. He writes to entertain. (Shakespeare also wrote to entertain, and he did it superbly; but he attempted and achieved much more.)

A writer might intend to entertain, to persuade, to stir emotion, or to inform—any or all of these are valid goals. The technical writer, however, focuses on just one goal—to inform. He describes, informs, or instructs with economy, accuracy, and clarity. He might even persuade if he is writing a brochure or a proposal for a contract, but his persuasion is through the objective information he presents. His goal is not to entertain. That is not to say that his writing is dull; if it is, he is not a good technical writer. But if the busy engineer, scientist, technician, or administrator for whom the writing is intended wants entertainment, he will look for it elsewhere and on his own time. From technical writings he wishes primarily to be informed—clearly, accurately, and sufficiently for his needs. In a sense, the technical writer is an interpreter, bringing intelligence and order to a vast array of raw data, and presenting the data in a usable form.

This book will not teach you how to write, although you might learn some things about the skill. If you already know how to express yourself in reasonably good, clear English, it will teach you to write more effectively on technical subjects. You will learn the elements of style that are peculiar to technical writing.

In addition to developing your technical writing skills, this book will teach you much more. It will help you learn how to get additional information on your subject. It describes the processes through which the written material must pass before it is ready to be printed and the facilities you may make use of in preparing your work.

As you work through this book, you will learn how to be critical of your own writing, and thus how to improve it; and at the end, you will find yourself on the way to becoming a more accurate, more concise, more informative—in short, more readable—writer. Which means a better writer.

Pacific Grove, California   Charles W. Ryan
September 1974

How to Use This Book

Much of the material in this book is in the form of programmed instruction, a technique that helps you learn more effectively by getting you directly involved in the material. Each bit (or frame) of programmed material is numbered. Have a pencil and an index card (or folded piece of paper) ready. When you reach a numbered frame, use the card to cover the answer below the dashed line. Read the question or instruction, do what is asked for in the frame, and then compare your answer with the one given. If you are correct, go ahead. If you make a mistake, be sure you understand the reason for your error before you go on.

Not everyone has the same problems with writing. Some of the material may seem too easy, but you will progress rapidly through these easy or familiar sections. When you reach sections that deal with your particular problems, slow down to make sure you thoroughly understand the material. Because the three Parts are self-contained, they need not be read in order. You can, if you wish, go directly to the Part that interests you.

Each chapter in Parts One and Two ends with a Self-Test to help you evaluate your mastery of the concepts presented. Before going on to the next chapter, take the Self-Test, compare your answers, and review the chapter if you missed many items.

Part Three presents samples of a variety of documents, with comments on particular elements of style. This Part is not programmed, since its only purpose is to provide you with additional information that you might find helpful.

An appendix presents a list of style guides and other useful books on writing.

Acknowledgments

I am grateful to the following people and organizations for their assistance and cooperation in preparing this book.

John Wiley & Sons, Inc. and the Wiley authors listed in the appendix for permission to use copyrighted material and pages from some internal publications.

Lockheed Missiles & Space Company, Inc., Sunnyvale, California, for permission to use selected pages from Lockheed documents as illustrations in this book.

Physics International Company, San Leandro, California, for blanket permission to select from its documents in illustrating the book.

Psychological Consultants, Inc., Richmond, Virginia, for permission to adapt selected material for illustrations in this book.

Parke, Davis & Company, Detroit, Michigan, for permission to use selected material, including portions of Effect of Ethanol on Intestinal Amino Acid Transport, by Tsun Chang and Anthony J. Glazko.

American Express Company and Fireman's Fund Insurance Company, for permission to use selected internal publications as illustrations.

Air Force Rocket Laboratory, Air Force Systems Command, Edwards Air Force Base, California, for the use of Cold Welding Research, Phase I Report, AFRPL-TR-211, January 1969, by D. B. Sheldon and W. T. Picciano.

Wanda Price, Manager of the Publications Department, Physics International Company, for invaluable assistance.

Herald Printers, Monterey, California, for the preparation of illustrations for publication.

John A. Walter of the University of Texas at Austin, Harold E. Daubert of the Westinghouse Corporation, and David W. Ewing of the Harvard Business Review, for reviewing the manuscript and offering many helpful suggestions.

Irene Brownstone, Programmed Instruction Editor at Wiley, for enormous help in preparing the manuscript.

Contents

Part One   WRITING PROCEDURES   1

Chapter 1   ORGANIZING THE WRITING   2

Discusses how to plan the written material, considering the purpose for which it is being written, the intended audience, the requirements that must be met, and the preparation of an outline.

Chapter 2   RESEARCHING THE WRITING   23

Describes the sources of information from which the writer works and explains how to research the writing through schematics, conferences with technical experts, examination of the hardware, engineering drawings, analysis of similar publications, and other research sources.

Chapter 3   STYLE   30

Explains how to select a format and how to use language and punctuation clearly and consistently. Shows how to handle headings, listings, tables, illustrations, standard abbreviations, and other mechanics of writing.

Chapter 4   TECHNICAL REVIEW   88

Deals with the ways a writer insures accuracy and clarity by individual conferences with technical experts, by the preparation of review copies of the work, and by the formal technical review.

Chapter 5   PRODUCTION   96

Outlines all steps in the publishing process
from rough draft to the final printer's package,
including the techniques of preparing graphic
material—photographs, drawings, tables,
charts, and graphs—as well as the functions
of the technical typists, editors, print shop,
and others contributing to the final document.

Chapter 6   PREPARING THE PRINTER'S PACKAGE   105

Follows the entire procedure from typing the
final manuscript to printing the document.
Discusses handling of graphic materials, providing instructions for line and screened negatives, checking the final copy for errors or
omissions, supervising the preparation of front
matter, coordinating with the print shop, preparing a printer's dummy, and attending to other
details necessary to produce the final printed
document.

Part Two   EFFECTIVE WRITING   117

Chapter 7   GRAMMAR   118

Covers some of the fundamentals of grammar
as applied to writing in business and industry.
This short chapter is intended more as review
than as basic instruction.

Chapter 8   EDITING   130

Presents editing symbols which are useful to a
writer, whether he is his own editor or (more
commonly) his work is edited by someone else.

Chapter 9   WRITING FUNCTIONAL SENTENCES   143

Focuses on sound sentence structure, presenting
the special style, requirements, and limitations
of writing for business and industry. Stressing
usefulness, accuracy, and clarity, this chapter
deals with the passive versus the active voice,
nouns used as adjectives, misuse of modifiers,
illogical shifts in sentence structure, and other
basic elements of functional sentences.

Chapter 10   WORDS AND PHRASES   166

Discusses how to avoid some ill-chosen words
and phrases that pervade writing in business
and industry: officialese, wordiness, and
cumbersome phrases.

Part Three   BASIC DOCUMENTS   191

Chapters 11 through 18 present some principal
documents that are common throughout business
and industry, describing the style, format, and
basic approach to each.

Chapter 11   MANUALS   192

Chapter 12   RESEARCH REPORTS   204

Chapter 13   PROGRESS REPORTS   214

Chapter 14   BROCHURES   221

Chapter 15   SPECIFICATIONS   230

Chapter 16   PROPOSALS   234

Chapter 17   ABSTRACTS   239

Chapter 18   TRANSMITTAL LETTERS   242

APPENDIX   245

INDEX   255

PART ONE
Writing Procedures

Part One deals with some of the routine procedures a writer must perform in preparing technical publications. It provides information that is essentially independent of the writing itself.

Every writer needs to know some of the material in Part One; however, some of the chapters may be of interest only in understanding what someone else does before the material is published.

Part One will help you to:

- research your writing;

- organize your writing project, deciding what you plan to cover and the audience you plan to write for;

- understand the basic elements of style to achieve consistency in format, language, and punctuation;

- plan for review of your material for technical accuracy;

- understand the procedures involved in the publication of your material;

- understand how the final manuscript is assembled for publication and how to coordinate the work of other departments, such as graphic arts, technical typing, and the print shop.

CHAPTER ONE
Organizing the Writing

When you finish this chapter you will be able to:

- decide the real purpose of your writing;
- direct your writing to its intended readers;
- prepare a workable outline.

The most agonizing time for you, the writer, is that initial period when you sit staring at a blank sheet of paper, waiting for the words to come. Eventually they do come, but you may waste a lot of time and effort before the words make sense. After many false starts and much rewriting, you finally arrange your thoughts in some kind of reasonable order and state them clearly, accurately, and completely.

Of course, you might not waste much time before you find yourself well on the way to communicating with your reader (which is what writing is all about). If this is true, it is probably because you did a good job of organizing your writing in the first place.

1. You can't hope to write, in any meaningful sense, unless you know the real purpose of your writing. Remember, we are talking about technical writing. In general, would you say the purpose of technical

    writing is to entertain? _____

    - - - - - - - - - - - - - - -

    You might, but I wouldn't! Of course, your writing shouldn't be dull, either.

2. Is the purpose of technical writing to stir the emotions? _____

    - - - - - - - - - - - - - - -

    I hope not. (You may arouse anger or frustration if you don't do a good job!)

3. Is the purpose of technical writing to present information?

_____

- - - - - - - - - - - - - - - -

Yes. This is the primary purpose of all technical writing. Even in the case of a proposal, written in the hope of getting a contract, or a brochure, written to sell goods or services, the persuasion is indirect. If the reader is persuaded, it is because the factual infor- mation is presented in a convincing manner.

4. The first three frames were just warmup exercises, because you probably knew, even if you never expressed it, that the business of the technical writer is to convey information. Your main problems in organizing your writing are, first of all, to decide what you are to write about and who is going to read what you write.

You have to be specific in answering the what. It is not enough, for example, to say you're going to write about the wheel. You have to ask yourself (or someone else) some further questions. Are you going to describe the physical appearance and construction of the wheel, tell how it works, explain how to make it last longer, or per- haps all these things and more? Before you can answer the what,

you also have to know something about the _____.

- - - - - - - - - - - - - - - -

who (or reader, or an equivalent answer)

5. Suppose your company manufactures high-voltage power supplies. Here are some of the documents you (or someone else in your com- pany) might have to write.

A maintenance manual

A manufacturer's installation instruction booklet

A brochure giving the price, applications, and electrical charac- teristics of the power supply

Which of these documents is likely to be of least value to the tech- nicians who might have to repair the power supply?

_____

- - - - - - - - - - - - - - - -

The brochure

6.   Which document would be most useful to the technicians?

_____

- - - - - - - - - - - - - - - -

The maintenance manual (although the installation instructions might be of some value to a technician who knew a lot about power supplies)

7.   Of the following people, who would be most likely to find the brochure useful?

A design engineer who is looking for a power supply with specific characteristics

The head of the purchasing department of a company that manufactures electrical equipment

The Contract Officer of a nearby Air Force base

_____

- - - - - - - - - - - - - - - -

The design engineer

8.   The installation instruction booklet would be most useful to the

people who _____ it.
                (design/install/repair)

- - - - - - - - - - - - - - - -

install

9.   Clearly, in planning a technical document, you must carefully consider who is going to read or use it. Now let's go back and take another look at that proposed maintenance manual for a high–voltage power supply. Who will be the user of that document?

_____

- - - - - - - - - - - - - - - -

The technician who must maintain the power supply (or words to that effect)

10. After you decide you are writing for a technician, what other important question must you answer before you begin to organize the manual?

_____

- - - - - - - - - - - - - - - -

What information to include in the manual (or an equivalent answer)

11. A maintenance manual is intended almost exclusively for the technician whose job is to keep the equipment in good working order. The equipment must be cleaned and inspected at intervals, and it must be repaired when something goes wrong. As the writer who will prepare this manual, let us assume that you already know these things about a technician's duties. Let us also assume that the high-voltage power supply is being built as you plan the manual, and the prototype has just been completed. You walk down to the fabrication area to look over the prototype, and you notice that there are some switches and other controls on the front panel. Thus, you realize that someone must operate the power supply. It now becomes clear to you that you must revise your thinking. What is your <u>full</u> purpose in writing the manual? _____

– – – – – – – – – – – – – – – – –

To tell how to maintain <u>and operate</u> the power supply

12. For the sake of simplicity, we'll assume that our high-voltage power supply has no large components that require mechanical adjustment or maintenance. Like all power supplies, it has various electrical components: transformers, rectifiers (vacuum tubes, selenium wafers, or something else), fuses, relays, resistors, and capacitors. The front panel has a main power switch, a potentiometer for adjusting voltage output, and a voltmeter for measuring output voltage. A technician must operate as well as maintain the power supply. Read over the following list of topics and put a check beside each one that you feel would need to be included in your operation and maintenance manual.

    Theoretical explanation of rectification (how alternating current is changed to direct current)

    Electrical circuit description

    Replacement parts list

    Troubleshooting tables (malfunction analysis)

    Inspection and cleaning instructions

    Instructions for installation and removal of components

    Use of special test equipment, if any

    Operation of front panel controls

– – – – – – – – – – – – – – – – –

You should probably include everything on the list except the theoretical explanation of rectification (the technician might know this, but he doesn't really need to). Of course, there might be additional topics that should be included.

13. Assume that you are employed by a company that manufactures house paints. You have been assigned to write a pamphlet, to be given away to retail customers, which explains how to perform a number of routine painting jobs in the home. One section of the pamphlet contains instructions for painting a door. Read the following list of topics and put a check beside each one that you feel should be included in your instructions.

Removing the old paint

Selecting the color

Preparing the surface

Choosing the brush

Protecting the hardware (doorknob, hinges)

Choosing the type of paint

Technique of painting

Cleaning the brush

- - - - - - - - - - - - - - - - -

You probably would not include "selecting the color," and "cleaning the brush" might be beyond the scope of your pamphlet. "Choosing the type of paint" is important, because different kinds of paint are used for doors in different locations. All the other topics are definitely related to the instructions for painting a door. You can probably think of a few more topics, especially if you have ever painted a door!

Note: The point of this frame is not to test your knowledge of door-painting but to remind you that you have to think through your subject, keeping in mind the needs of your readers.

14. Your decisions about who will use a document and what it should include depend upon the type of document. This chapter is not so much concerned with what your decisions should be as with how the decisions are made. Brochures, proposals, reports, and other types of technical documents are discussed in detail in other chapters. Once you decide who will read your document and what it should contain, you are ready to think about an outline. On the next page, place a check beside the phrase that you feel describes the main purpose of an outline.

To help you decide the purposes you hope to accomplish in your document

To enable you to plan the actual writing

— — — — — — — — — — — — — — — —

To enable you to plan the actual writing. The outline might also remind you to include additional material, or it might lead you to eliminate some topics.

15. Since you are likely to know already the subject you are dealing with in your writing, the hardest part of the writing might be the preparation of an outline. But you must make an outline for anything more ambitious than the briefest of reports (even then you should have a mental outline). The outline makes any writing easier and, more important, more successful. Without it, you flounder in trying to write, and your reader struggles in trying to make sense out of what you have written.

    Since the outline is the plan of your writing, there are two major factors to consider in developing it. Thinking back over outlines you have written or examined, you probably realize that you have to decide what subject matter to include and the order in which to present it. In frame 12 you examined a list of topics to try to decide what should be included in your operation and maintenance manual. In preparing your outline, this list is part of the process of establishing the subject matter to be included. The other major step is

    to decide _____.

— — — — — — — — — — — — — — — —

the order in which the material should be arranged (or an equivalent answer).

16. The order in which the material is presented depends upon the subject matter and the type of document you are writing. Here are some of the ways you might decide to order your presentation. *

    Time

    Place

    Increasing importance

    Decreasing importance

    Best effect

---

*These orders are somewhat modified from the orders of presentation discussed in detail in Effective Writing: For Engineers, Managers, Scientists by H. J. Tichy (New York: John Wiley & Sons, 1966).

Which of these orders would you choose in making an outline of a report on the day-to-day and month-to-month progress of an election campaign? _____

– – – – – – – – – – – – – – – – –

The order of time seems most logical. Time, or chronological order, is used very often in all kinds of documents, sometimes even when another order might be better!

17. Continue to refer to the list in frame 16 for the next few frames. A great many technical reports are devoted to problem solving. Here is a simple outline for this type of report.

> Short Summary
>
> Statement of Problem
>
> Analysis of Problem
>
> Description of Proposed Solutions
>
> Advantages and Disadvantages of Proposed Solutions
>
> Conclusions and Recommendations

Which of the orders listed in frame 16 seems to be applicable to this outline? _____

– – – – – – – – – – – – – – – – –

Order of best effect
    Note: In this order of outlining, it is important to place each topic where it will do the reader the most good. For example, you have to know what the problem is before you can consider solutions. A short summary came first in this outline because many busy men and women spend entirely too much time reading paperwork. The summary tells the reader whether he needs to go further into the report.

18. Sometimes a report is organized so that less important material comes first, followed by increasingly important information until the climax of the report is reached. This is, of course, the order of increasing importance. Newspaper reporters learn to write their articles to meet something called the "clip test." Because the space available for a story is quite variable, the item should be written for clipping from the bottom, if necessary, to make room. It naturally follows that material likely to be clipped should not be very important. The most important information is in the first sentence or two.

Such a "clip test" organization follows an order of _____

_____.

– – – – – – – – – – – – – – – –

decreasing importance

19. A market analysis that presents the results of research in a number of widely separated geographical locations might be organized with

an order of _____.

– – – – – – – – – – – – – – –

place

20. Which order listed in frame 16 do you think would be best for our

operation and maintenance manual?   _____

– – – – – – – – – – – – – – – –

Order of best effect
    Note: There might be some other effective order, but not in the list in frame 16. With the orders discussed in the last few frames, the labels are not important and the categories are certainly not holy. The important point is that you recognize the many ways to organize your material, and that you realize you should choose the most effective organization for your document and for your readers.

21. Fortunately, you very often do not have to start "from scratch." Since all kinds of technical documents are filed in your company's technical library, or in its publication section, there is one way you can get a lot of help in planning your outline. What is it?

_____

_____

– – – – – – – – – – – – – – –

Examine similar documents to see how they are organized. (For example, your company might have published manuals on other electrical equipment. Even if it has not produced a manual on a power supply, the organization of your manual would be similar to that for other electrical equipment. But be careful. Many published documents are poorly organized, so you have to examine critically.)

22. Dr. Hardy Hoover* suggests four rules for preparing an outline:

    a. Include every topic required by the subject.

    b. Exclude every topic not required by the subject.

    c. Working from the top down, divide each topic into all its subordinates.

    d. Order each group of coordinates properly.

To clarify the meaning of the terms subordinate and coordinate, assume you are writing a paper about domestic produce. Two obvious coordinate, or roughly equal, topics are "fruits" and "vegetables." Two topics under "fruits" might be "apples" and "pears." These are coordinate topics, but they are subordinate to "fruits." Taking your outline one step further, "Anjou pears" and "Bartlett pears" are possible coordinate topics that are subordinate to "pears," while "Delicious apples" and "Winesap apples" are possible coordinate topics that are subordinate to "apples."

Let's plan a report entitled "Fundamentals of Arithmetic" and see how Dr. Hoover's first two rules are applied. Examine the tentative outline below.

    I.   Addition

    II.   Subtraction

    III. Multiplication

    IV. Simple Equations

Does the outline include every topic required by the subject? If not, what is missing? _____

– – – – – – – – – – – – – – – –

"Division," a necessary topic, has been left out. You might also wish to include "Fractions."

23. Does the outline include a topic that should be excluded? If so, what is it? _____

– – – – – – – – – – – – – – – –

"Simple Equations" should be excluded. It is a topic in algebra, not in arithmetic.

_____

*Hardy Hoover, Essentials for the Technical Writer (New York: John Wiley & Sons, 1970).

24. The following outline gives the primary topics for a report called "The Planets of the Solar System."

    I.   Mercury

    II.   Venus

    III.   Moon

    IV.   Mars

    V.   Jupiter

    VI.   Saturn

    VII. Uranus

    VIII. Neptune

    IX.   Pluto

What topic required by the subject has been left out? _____

_____

— — — — — — — — — — — — — — — —

Earth is a planet of the solar system. You might have considered the asteroid belt an omission, too.

25. What topic included in the outline should be excluded? _____

_____

— — — — — — — — — — — — — — — —

Moon. The moon is a satellite, not a planet.

26. Dr. Hoover's third rule is: Working from the top down, divide each topic into all its subordinates. Now things get a little more complicated. In outlining our report on "The Planets of the Solar System," we dealt only with primary headings. Jupiter is a lot bigger than Mercury, but they are both equally planets of the solar system. We can't break these primary headings down into subordinate headings because of the way we started our outline. But we might have had different primary headings; for example, the ones below could be used.

    I.   Inner Planets

    II.   Outer Planets

If you are shaky on astronomy, don't worry about it. The asteroid belt is a conventional boundary, so the primary and secondary headings might look like those on the next page.

I. Inner Planets

    A. Mercury

    B. Venus

    C. Earth

    D. Mars

II. Outer Planets

    A. Jupiter

    B. Saturn

    C. Uranus

    D. Neptune

    E. Pluto

It is difficult to find subjects to outline without immediately falling into differences of opinion about how the subordinate topics should be arranged. We will try one subject that should find general agreement. (Of course, we can't agree on what to say about the subordinates!) Fill in the blanks in the following outline.

The Numbers 1 through 10

I. _____

    A. _____

    B. _____

    C. _____

    D. 7

    E. 9

II. _____

    A. _____

    B. 4

    C. _____

    D. 8

    E. _____

— — — — — — — — — — — — — —

I. Odd numbers
    A. 1
    B. 3
    C. 5
    D. 7
    E. 9
II. Even numbers
    A. 2
    B. 4
    C. 6
    D. 8
    E. 10

27. Of course, each topic need not have the same number of subordinate headings. You use as many as necessary to cover the subject. It might be that some primary topics have no subordinates. In arithmetic, it is easy to see that division might be broken down into long division and short division, but it is not so easy to decide whether addition, subtraction, and multiplication have such subordinates.

    In the space below, make an outline for a report entitled "Current Coins of the United States" in which your primary headings are "Silver Coins" and "Non-Silver Coins." Include all the subordinate headings you feel are necessary.

- - - - - - - - - - - - - - - - - -

I. Silver Coins
    A. Silver dollar
    B. Half dollar
    C. Quarter
    D. Dime
II. Non-Silver Coins
    A. Nickel
    B. Penny
    Note: You might have had a somewhat different arrangement, such as putting non-silver coins first or reversing the order of values.

28. Dr. Hoover's fourth rule is: Order each group of coordinates properly. So now we must be sure we understand the terms <u>subordinates</u> and <u>coordinates</u>. If two topics are coordinates, are they equal or unequal in rank? (Hint: "Silver Coins" and "Non-Silver Coins" are coordinate topics in frame 27.) _____

- - - - - - - - - - - - - - - -

They are equal in rank. (No one suggested they were equal in actual value, but they are both primary headings in the outline.)

29. Name a subordinate topic under the primary heading "Silver Coins."

_____

- - - - - - - - - - - - - - - -

Silver dollar, half dollar, etc.

30. Name a subordinate topic under the primary heading "Pacific Coast States." _____

- - - - - - - - - - - - - - - -

California, Oregon, or Washington

31. Judging from the examples in frame 29, you can see that a topic might be both subordinate and coordinate, depending on what it is being related to. "Silver dollar" and "half dollar" are subordinate topics to "Silver Coins," but they are coordinate with each other.

Is "silver dollar" also coordinate with "nickel"? _____

- - - - - - - - - - - - - - - -

Yes. They are both secondary headings. "Silver dollar" is subordinate to "Silver Coins," and "nickel" is subordinate to "Non-Silver Coins," but they are coordinate at the second level.

32. In ordering each group of coordinates properly, you must be logical and consistent. For example, you would not list "shilling" under "Silver Coins" in our outline, because a shilling is not a United States coin. Look at the outline fragment on the next page. Below the partial outline, write what you think is wrong with it.

I.   Pacific Coast States

   A. Baja California

   B. California

   C. Oregon

   D. Washington

   E. British Columbia

Perhaps nothing. You need to know the <u>subject</u> of the complete outline. If you assumed that the primary heading meant Pacific coast
states of the United States, then you would say that Baja California
and British Columbia don't belong in the outline. But Baja California
is a state of Mexico, and it's on the Pacific coast. And British
Columbia, also on the Pacific coast, is called a province but in a
sense it is a state of Canada. This was not intended as a trick
question. If you eliminated A and E, it merely shows one way of
reasoning.

33. Your outline should preserve <u>parallelism</u> as much as possible. That
is, subject matter which occurs under one major heading should be
treated about equally under similar headings. Supply the missing
portions in this outline fragment.

I.   Pacific Coast States

   A. California

      1. History

      2. Principal Industries

      3. Recreation Areas

   B. Oregon

      1. _____

      2. _____

      3. _____

----

1. History; 2. Principal Industries; 3. Recreation Areas. (You
would include the same subordinate topics under "C. Washington.")

34. In the case of our Pacific coast states, perfect parallelism can be maintained, because whatever you can discuss about one state you can discuss about another—at least, in the earlier stages. You have to use your own judgment. "Cotton Production" might be a topic listed under "Principal Industries" for California, but if Washington produces any cotton at all, it is certainly not a principal industry.

    Following is the beginning of an outline for a report called "NATO Armies." In the space provided, add at least one more primary heading with its subordinate headings.

    I. Great Britain

    A. Troop strength

    B. Geographical distribution

- - - - - - - - - - - - - - - - - -

    II. France (or Norway, or any other NATO country)
    A. Troop strength
    B. Geographical distribution

35. Sometimes you have to settle for <u>equivalence</u> rather than <u>parallelism</u> in your outline. In discussing the utilities in a home, you might have to describe the electrical system, the plumbing system, and the gas system. You would go into about the same amount of detail for each system, but the information would not be parallel, because electricity, gas, and water have different properties and are handled differently. Here is a portion of an outline involving these systems. Fill in the blanks.

    I. Electrical System

    A. Wiring

    B. Switches

    C. Receptacles

    II. Plumbing System

    A. _____

    B. _____

    C. _____

- - - - - - - - - - - - - - - -

A. Piping; B. Valves; C. Faucets (or Outlets, etc.)

36. The following paragraph contains information on operating a camera; the poorly arranged presentation is deliberate. In the space provided, outline a report entitled "How to Operate a Camera" using the information given.

The aperture, which lets the light pass through the lens to the film, can be varied. The various sizes of openings are called "f-stops." The camera must be focused to be sure the image on the film is sharp. Focusing is done by varying the distance between the lens and the film. The length of time the film is exposed to the light is controlled by the shutter speed, which can be varied. The exposure of the film to the light can be controlled by varying either the shutter speed or the aperture, since both affect the amount of light admitted when the picture is taken. There is a definite relationship between f-stop (size of aperture) and shutter speed. A good memory aid for checking all steps in taking a picture is SAFE, which stands for "shutter, aperture, focus, and exposure." The exposure of the film occurs when the shutter is triggered. The length of exposure depends on the type of film used.

Here is one simple outline that is based on the information. Yours will no doubt differ in some ways.

I.   SAFE Approach to Operating a Camera
   A.   Shutter
   B.   Aperture
   C.   Focus
   D.   Exposure
II. Shutter
   A.   Shutter speed
   B.   Relationship to aperture
III. Aperture
   A.   What are f-stops?
   B.   Relationship of aperture to shutter speed
IV. Focus
V.   Exposure
   A.   Relationship of light to film speed
   B.   Triggering of shutter

Note: If you included topics in your outline that were not in the given information, you were actually benefiting from one purpose of an outline, which is to remind you to say everything that needs saying. No information was given about how to set shutter speed and aperture, how to focus the camera, or how to trigger the shutter. Obviously, your reader would need to know these things before he or she could operate a camera.

37. Everyone is familiar with the various states of water: liquid, steam, the various manifestations of ice, as in snow, sleet, or hail, and the suspension of tiny droplets to form clouds. While you might not remember all the details of how the various states of water are brought about, you certainly know enough to allow yourself to try an outline of a short report entitled "The States of Water." Use the next page to write such an outline, and then compare it with mine on page 20.

The States of Water
I.   The Solid State
    A.   What is Ice?
        1.   Freezing Temperature
        2.   Physical Characteristics
    B.   Various Forms of Ice
        1.   "Ordinary" Ice
            a.   Description
            b.   Formation
        2.   Hail
            a.   Description
            b.   Formation
        3.   Snow
            a.   Description
            b.   Formation
        4.   Sleet
            a.   Description
            b.   Formation
II.   The Liquid State
    A.   What is "Ordinary" Water?
        1.   Temperature Range
        2.   Physical Characteristics
    B.   What is Water Vapor?
        1.   Definition of a Cloud
        2.   Difference Between Water Vapor and Steam
III.   The Gaseous State
    A.   What is Steam?
        1.   Temperature Range
        2.   Physical Characteristics

Note: Obviously, your outline can be quite different from mine. You might check to see that you cover the same subjects, where possible, under each of your coordinate headings.

SELF-TEST

The following questions will test your understanding of Chapter 1.
Answers are provided on the following page.

1.   What is the main purpose of technical writing? _____

_____

2.   In planning your writing, you must make two major decisions before
     you start to prepare your outline.   What are they?

     (a) _____

     (b) _____

3.   Five different orders of presentation were discussed in this chapter.

     Name three of them.   _____

_____

4.   Following is a paragraph with information on building a campfire;
     the poorly arranged presentation is deliberate.   On a separate piece
     of paper, outline a report entitled "How to Build a Campfire" using
     the information given.

          The wood should be dry and will have to be of different
     sizes.   Kindling is required to start the fire, and this may
     be either paper or wood shavings.   Small pieces of wood
     have to be arranged above the kindling, since if only large
     wood is used, the kindling might quit burning before the
     fire catches.   The site of the fire bed should be dry.   It
     might be lined with stones, but it is important that there
     be a good venting arrangement to furnish a draft for the
     fire.   The wood should be arranged with spaces in between
     for good venting.   The kindling goes on the bottom, with
     the small wood intermediate, and then the logs or other
     large wood.   It is assumed that one will have either a
     lighter or matches.   The use of flint and steel and other
     fire-making techniques are beyond the scope of this
     report.

Answers to Self-Test

If your answers to the test questions do not agree with the ones given below, review the frames indicated in parentheses after each answer before you go on to the next chapter.

1. The main purpose of technical writing is to provide information. (frame 3)

2. You have to decide who is going to read your writing and what should be included. (frames 9 and 10)

3. The five orders of presentation given in the chapter are: time, place, increasing importance, decreasing importance, and best effect. (frame 16)

4. Here is a possible outline from the information given. Yours is probably different, but at least check it against the original, unorganized material to be sure you covered everything.

    How to Build a Campfire

    I. Fuel
        A. Kindling
            1. Paper
            2. Wood shavings
        B. Fire Wood
            1. Intermediate
            2. Large wood
    II. Preparing a Campfire Site
        A. Preparing a Fire Bed
        B. Arranging for a Draft
    III. Building the Fire
        A. Arranging the Fuel
        B. Igniting the Fire

    (frame 36)

CHAPTER TWO
Researching the Writing

When you finish this chapter you will be able to:

- define your research requirements;
- identify your sources of information.

How much research do you need to do before you begin your writing? That depends on how much you know. If you must write a maintenance manual for a piece of sophisticated machinery, the research task might be enormous. If you are a sales manager preparing a report on the feasibility of expanding certain territories, you might already have your general arguments in mind and need only to research the details—the facts and figures. But unless you have almost perfect knowledge of your subject and a talent for total recall, you must do some research. In researching your writing, you need to ask yourself three basic questions:

What do I need to know?

What are the sources of information available to me?

How do I use those sources to extract the information I require?

1.   At what point are you able to decide, in a general way, what you need to know for your writing project? Place a check beside the correct answer.

When you are assigned, or when you assign yourself, the writing project.

When you have completed your outline.

When you revise your first draft.

– – – – – – – – – – – – – – – –

When you have completed your outline. Only when you have established what will be included in your writing can you decide what you already know and what you must find out. Sometimes you will find, as a result of your research, that you need to change your outline to include or exclude material. Remember that the outline should be flexible—it is a guide, not a law.

2. A business letter is very often a form of technical writing. Would you ever need to do any research in writing business letters?

_____

– – – – – – – – – – – – – – – –

Yes. Suppose you need to answer a letter that begins, "Please send a list of delivery dates for the transformers to be supplied under Contract CH-40879-21." Even if you recognized the contract number, would you be willing to trust your memory for the dates?

3. How would you get the information to answer the question about delivery dates? _____

– – – – – – – – – – – – – – – –

Probably you would either look up the delivery dates in the contract or pick up the telephone and ask someone.

4. Background information is often necessary for you to grasp the material about which you intend to write, and it is easy to locate bibliographies on a vast array of technical subjects. Rather than grope around hoping to stumble upon useful information, seek out the person in charge of the technical library for your company and ask for help in identifying the best sources of information for your subject. Almost every company has a technical library of some kind. It might occupy a whole floor and employ several fulltime librarians, or it might be a small part of one room. You might also look for information in a nearby community or college library.

As indicated in frame 3, two important sources of information are written materials and _____.

– – – – – – – – – – – – – – – –

people

5. Don't assume that all the written sources of information are printed or published. Suppose you are a physicist, and you are planning to write a paper on your series of experiments with charged particles.

You must look up exact data in producing your paper. Where would
you look? _____

- - - - - - - - - - - - - - - -

In your notebooks, computer printouts, or anywhere else that you
recorded exact data resulting from your experiments.

6. When we mentioned printed materials a little earlier, we did not
   mean words only. That high-voltage power supply we talked about
   in Chapter 1 generated a lot of paper before it was completed.
   Documents necessary for its production included:

   > Engineering drawings, or blueprints, showing the exact
   > physical description of each individual part as well as
   > assembly drawings showing how all those parts are put
   > together.

   > Wiring diagrams to show the exact position of the elec-
   > trical wiring, plugs, and connectors.

   > Schematic diagrams, which show the electrical operation
   > of circuits but not their physical appearance or location.

   If you want to study the electrical operation of a piece of equipment,
   which of these would you study? Check the answer.

   > Assembly drawings

   > Wiring diagrams

   > Schematic diagrams

- - - - - - - - - - - - - - - -

Schematic diagrams. The others show only physical characteristics,
not electrical.

7. The word <u>schematic</u> means that symbols are used to represent components, with lines showing electrical but not physical relationships.
   If you are studying a module and want to know the physical routing of

   the main power leads, you should consult a _____ diagram.

- - - - - - - - - - - - - - - -

wiring. A schematic diagram does not show physical locations.

8. The last two frames were not really intended to teach you anything
   about electrical equipment. You might not know anything about
   electricity. Suppose you don't, but you find that you must understand

some very basic electrical facts in writing a paper about something that is largely mechanical. You don't have time to study a course in basic electricity and have no idea how to read schematic diagrams. Write in one sentence what you would do to gain your information.

— — — — — — — — — — — — — — — —

Find someone who knows and ask him (or an equivalent response).

9. As you have seen, written materials and knowledgeable people are important research sources. Of course, there is a third which is so obvious that it might not immediately occur to you. Care to guess?

_____

— — — — — — — — — — — — — — — —

Your personal observation or experience (or equivalent).

10. After years of experience as an office manager and then personnel manager, you decide to write a manual of office procedures. Of the following research sources, which do you think would be most helpful in this project? Check the answer.

Sample office procedures manuals from other companies

A book entitled How to Write an Office Procedures Manual

Your own experience

— — — — — — — — — — — — — — — —

Your own experience. The other sources might be very valuable, but your own knowledge and background will help most in dealing with your exact situation.

11. What are the three major research sources? _____

_____

— — — — — — — — — — — — — — — —

Written materials, other people, and your own knowledge and experience.

12. In preparing a maintenance manual, you find it necessary to write a procedure for disassembly and assembly of a mechanical device. Complete engineering drawings are available, as well as a technician familiar with the device, the engineer who designed it, and the device

itself. Which of the following methods of research would you use in writing the procedure? Write the letter or letters in the space provided.

(a) Study the drawings to familiarize yourself with all the parts and how they are put together.

(b) Consult with the engineer, before or during your writing, as well as afterwards (to review it).

(c) Ask the technician to disassemble and assemble the device while you observe and take notes.

(d) Disassemble and assemble the device yourself, writing the procedure as you go.

Surely you would make some use of (a) and (b). In addition, it would be advisable to do either (c) or (d), or perhaps both, depending on your own ability and inclination. I would study the drawings, then attempt the procedure myself, using the drawings as a guide. If I needed help, I would ask the technician. Finally, I would go through the entire procedure again, following my written instructions exactly, but revising the procedure if it appeared necessary. Finally, I would give the procedure to the design engineer for his review and comments.

SELF-TEST

These questions will test your understanding of Chapter 2. Answers are provided following the test.

1. The first question you should ask yourself in researching your writing

    is _____.

2. List the three major research sources.

    _____

    _____

    _____

3. A useful source of information on many technical subjects is your

    company's _____.

4. If you can't find your information in written materials, you can

    usually locate _____.

5. One of your best sources of information on subjects in your own

    field is _____.

6. The best way to learn and then test a detailed procedure is to

    _____.

Answers to Self-Test

If your answers to the test questions do not agree with the ones given below, review the frames indicated in parentheses after each answer before you go on to the next chapter.

1. What do I need to know? or something similar. (frame 1)

2. Written materials, other people, and your own knowledge and experience. (frames 4, 5, 8, 9, 10, and 11)

3. technical library. (frame 4)

4. someone who knows. (frames 3, 8, 11, and 12)

5.   yourself (or words to that effect).   (frames 9 and 10)

6.   do it yourself (or observe someone else doing it).   (frame 12)

CHAPTER THREE
Style

When you finish this chapter you will be able to:

- identify the basic <u>elements</u> of style;
- select a <u>format</u> for a particular writing project;
- follow consistent usage in <u>language</u>;
- <u>punctuate</u> clearly and consistently.

The original title of this chapter was "Style and Format," although format is actually one element of style. You will find that many people speak of style and format as if they were separate and parallel subjects. Perhaps this is because format is a very mechanical thing, and thus easy to grasp, while the other elements of style are more subtle.

Style is concerned with the manner in which you present your information, not the content. The following two sentences illustrate what I mean.

The author is aware that the reader might find style hard to define.

I am aware that you might find style hard to define.

It is not wrong to avoid personal pronouns (although I know people who think it is wrong to use them in formal writing), but I prefer the style of the second sentence for this book. Most readers, unless they have been conditioned to think otherwise, would probably agree.

The next two sentences illustrate a more subtle example of style.

Many usages must be followed simply because they are "standard."

Many usages must be followed simply because they are "standard".

Again, I prefer the second sentence, because I think it is more logical in dealing with anything less than a complete sentence in quotation marks. But if I placed the period outside the quotes in my manuscript, I would merely make more work for my editors, who would move the period inside the quotes throughout the manuscript. The editors are not less logical than I am; it is just that this particular usage is so standardized that few editors care to violate it.

If you master the fundamentals of good style, you will make things easier for your readers, and you will make your writing task simpler. Because you have developed <u>standard</u> ways of presenting your information, you can get on with the <u>information</u> itself.

BASIC ELEMENTS OF STYLE

1. We are not concerned in this chapter with literary style; it is doubt-ful if that can be taught. Rather, we are interested in editorial style, which can be learned much more easily. Style encompasses everything related to the presentation of the written language on the page, and nothing more. So please do not take anything in this chapter as gospel. There are almost infinite variations in "correct" punctuation and other elements of style. Guidelines are offered, but your departures from the guidelines may be equally correct.
   Read the following sentence aloud.

   He drove the 2-ton truck from Memphis, Tenn. to
   Mobile, Ala.

   Now read this sentence aloud.

   He drove the two-ton truck from Memphis, Tennessee
   to Mobile, Alabama.

   Did the two sentences sound alike when read aloud? _____
   _ _ _ _ _ _ _ _ _ _ _ _ _ _ _
   They should have sounded exactly alike.

2. Draw a line under everything in the second sentence below that is different from something in the first sentence.

   he said have you seen my twelve inch ruler

   He said, "Have you seen my 12-inch ruler?"

   _ _ _ _ _ _ _ _ _ _ _ _ _ _

He said, "Have you seen my 12-inch ruler?"

The style of the Self-Teaching Guides is quite different from the style of most technical writing, particularly in the arrangement of section and paragraph headings. Therefore, a "Summary of Style," as it might be presented in a technical report, is shown in Figure 3-1, Sheets 1 and 2, on pages 34 and 35. Read through the summary now. You will need to refer to it frequently later in the chapter.

The three basic elements of style are format, language, and punctuation.

Format is concerned with the arrangement of text (or other matter) on the page. It includes the spacing of margins, the indentation of paragraphs, and the style of headings. It does not include the way words and phrases are written or how they are punctuated.

Language has a special definition in this book. This element of style is sometimes called "terminology" or "mechanics." Language is concerned with the exact manner in which words and phrases are presented in writing. It includes abbreviations, capitalization, compounding, and other details of the written language. One might argue that punctuation falls within this definition. It does. But punctuation is important enough to be dealt with as a separate element, so I limit my definition of language even more: When you read a passage aloud, every word or phrase that you hear is included as language. Those details that you do not hear, except as voice inflections or pauses, are included in the element of punctuation. If my definition of language seems a bit arbitrary, so be it. But it does make the subject of style easier to deal with.

Punctuation, then, is that portion of the language that is written but not spoken. Punctuation marks such as commas, periods, and parentheses might be regarded as signposts that make understanding easier. The punctuation marks may be heard in the spoken language as pauses or voice inflections, but they are not heard as words. Some authorities regard capitalization as a detail of punctuation, but by my definitions, it is part of the way a word is presented and thus is language, not punctuation.

3. When you try to decide whether you should use a comma or a semicolon, are you considering a matter of format, language, or

punctuation? _____

_ _ _ _ _ _ _ _ _ _ _ _ _ _ _

punctuation

4. If you decide to spell out "percent" rather than use the symbol %,
    are you making a choice about format, language, or punctuation?

    _____

    _ _ _ _ _ _ _ _ _ _ _ _ _ _

    language

5. Examine two ways of arranging the same material.

    The survey was confined to three cities: New York,
    Chicago, and San Francisco.

    The survey was confined to three cities:
        1. New York
        2. Chicago
        3. San Francisco

    The main difference between the two arrangements is one of

    _____.
    (format/language/punctuation)

    _ _ _ _ _ _ _ _ _ _ _ _ _ _

    format

6. Which element of style is concerned with matters such as margins,
    headings, indentation, page numbers (pagination), and type styles?

    _____

    _ _ _ _ _ _ _ _ _ _ _ _ _

    format

7. Another element of style is concerned with capitalization, abbrevia-
    tion, compounding of words, spelling, and the use of symbols such

    as %, #, and °. Which is it? _____

    _ _ _ _ _ _ _ _ _ _ _ _ _

    language

8. Which element of style is concerned with the use of commas, semi-
    colons, colons, dashes, and similar devices?

    _____

    _ _ _ _ _ _ _ _ _ _ _ _ _

    punctuation

SUMMARY OF STYLE

This section is not only a summary of the basic elements of style; it is also an illustration of some details of format that are widely used in technical writing. Note the way distinctions are made among primary, secondary, and tertiary (third-order) headings.

3-1 DEFINITION OF STYLE

Style encompasses everything related to the presentation of the written language on the page, and nothing more.

3-2 BASIC ELEMENTS OF STYLE

The three basic elements of style are format, language, and punctuation. These three elements are defined below.

3-3 Format

Format is concerned with the *arrangement* of text (or other matter) on the page, such as the spacing of margins, indentation of paragraphs, and the style of headings.

3-4 Language

This element of style is sometimes called "terminology" or "mechanics." Language is concerned with the exact manner in which the language is presented in writing. It includes abbreviations, capitalization, compounding, and other details of the written language, but it does *not* include punctuation.

3-5 Capitalization. Proper nouns, titles, and other words to be capitalized are discussed at greater length in the programmed instruction.

3-6 Abbreviations. Abbreviations can be confusing because of conflicting usage. Although some abbreviations are standard, it's better to consult a style guide.

Figure 3-1 (Sheet 1). Summary of style.

SUMMARY OF STYLE (Continued)

3-7 Symbols. There is fairly wide agreement among authorities about the use of symbols in text. A symbol is the non-phonetic written presentation of a word or other concept.

3-8 Compounding. The compounding of words is a problem, because there are no firm rules for deciding how the elements of compounds are to be connected: with hyphens, with spaces, or with nothing.

3-9 Spelling. When there are alternative spellings, the technical writer is generally wise to choose the more modern spelling.

3-10 Punctuation

     Punctuation is that portion of the language that is written but *not spoken*. Punctuation marks such as commas, periods, and parentheses might be regarded as signposts that make understanding easier. The punctuation marks may be heard in the spoken language as pauses or voice inflections, but they are not heard as *words*.

3-11 Comma. The comma might indicate a pause, but it is also a visual aid to understanding.

3-12 Semicolon. The semicolon indicates a more definite separation between thoughts than a comma does.

3-13 Colon. The colon is a signal to the reader to note what follows.

3-14 Hyphen. The hyphen is a connecting symbol that is used to show a close relationship between words or word fragments.

Figure 3-1 (Sheet 2). Summary of style.

9. The two following examples represent a difference of style.

    Semicolon
    The semicolon is similar to the comma, but it represents
    a more significant break between thoughts or groups of

    Semicolon. The semicolon is similar to the comma, but
    it represents a more significant break between thoughts

    Which basic element of style is illustrated by the above examples?

    _____

    – – – – – – – – – – – – – – –

    format

10. The two following examples represent a difference of style.

    The 5-gallon can contained a mixture that was 25 percent
    water and 75 percent gasoline.

    The five-gallon can contained a mixture that was 25%
    water and 75% gasoline.

    Which basic element of style is illustrated by the above examples?

    _____

    – – – – – – – – – – – – – – –

    language

11. The two following examples represent a difference of style.

    We now import large quantities of certain critical re-
    sources. Oil is a prime example.

    We now import large quantities of certain critical re-
    sources; oil is a prime example.

    Which basic element of style is illustrated by the above examples?

    _____

    – – – – – – – – – – – – – – –

    punctuation

12. What are the three basic elements of style? _____

    _____

    – – – – – – – – – – – – – – –

format, language, and punctuation

13. The words are the same, but the style is different, in the fragments
of a letter below.

> Dear Mr. Jones,
>> You can expect 25% delivery of your order by Mar. 31.

> Dear Mr. Jones:
> You can expect 25 percent delivery of your order by
> March 31.

What basic elements of style differ in the two examples above?

_____

– – – – – – – – – – – – – – – –

all three: format, language, and punctuation

14. What is different about the format? _____

– – – – – – – – – – – – – – – –

indentation

15. What is different about the punctuation? _____

– – – – – – – – – – – – – – – –

the use of a comma after "Jones" in one example and a colon in
the other example

16. What is different about the language? _____

– – – – – – – – – – – – – – – –

the method of writing "percent" and the abbreviation of "March"

17. The technical writer is like a judge in one respect: He looks to the
past for guidance in current decisions. The judge looks for precedents in legal cases similar to the one he is judging, while the writer
looks for precedents in matters of style (in style guides, similar
documents, or his own experience) in making decisions about usage.
Several examples of differing styles have been presented in this
chapter. In each case, how did you decide what the differences were?

_____

– – – – – – – – – – – – – – – –

You compared the two examples in each case.

MASTERING THE ELEMENTS OF STYLE

The specific style usages presented in this book are largely standard throughout business and industry, but many companies have compiled their own style guides, which might differ in particulars from general usage. If your writing is mostly in one specific field, there might be a recommended style guide for your field. In electronics, for example, one widely accepted guide is that provided by the Institute of Electrical and Electronics Engineers (IEEE). You will find a list of style guides for specific professions in the appendix of this book.

A style guide regarded as the "bible" by many writers when their company style guides do not provide guidance is the U.S. Government Printing Office Style Manual.

Whatever style guide you select for guidance, or whatever your personal exceptions to that guide, one point is of great importance: You must be consistent throughout your manuscript in any particular usage. This often means that you have to check back from time to time to see exactly how you expressed something, particularly if you are following a style guide that is new to you.

Format

Format is mechanical and largely arbitrary. The variations are almost endless, although a great many standard usages have evolved. A good format will give your manuscript a professional appearance and lend authority to your presentation. It will also help your readers to grasp more easily the information you are presenting.

Format is concerned with the arrangement of text (or other matter) on the page. What spacing should you use for margins? How many spaces should you indent paragraphs? How will you distinguish between primary paragraph* headings and subordinate headings? Where will you place the page numbers?

The format you choose depends upon the material you are writing, the facilities available for typing and printing the final document, company standards, and many other things. Once you have selected a

---

*In technical writing, "paragraph" has more than one meaning. Look at Figure 3-1, Sheet 1. There is one indented paragraph under "3-2 BASIC ELEMENTS OF STYLE." There might have been several indented paragraphs (sometimes called "subparagraphs") but all the material under that heading would be called "paragraph 3-2." But if you refer to that paragraph elsewhere in text, the preferable style would be something like, "Refer to 3-2."

format, it is important for you to follow it consistently throughout the manuscript.

18. <u>Margins</u> should be consistent throughout a manuscript. Even though you may not be typing your manuscript or making the final preparations for printing it, you should be aware of the general standards. Usually the side margins of a typed page are equal in width to each other and to the top margin. The margin at the bottom of the page is slightly larger. For example, a typical manuscript might have 1-inch side margins, a 1-inch top margin, and a $1\frac{1}{2}$-inch bottom margin.

On a typed page would there be more space at the bottom than at the top? _____ Would the right-hand margin be equal to the left-hand margin? _____

_ _ _ _ _ _ _ _ _ _ _ _ _ _ _ _ _

Yes to both questions

19. Although we are not ready to talk about the actual printing of a technical document, another word about margins here might be helpful. Look at the pages you are now reading; in particular, notice the side margins of each page. Your eye is fooled by the binding of a book, which makes the outside margins appear to be greater than the inside (gutter) margins. On the left-hand page, the left margin is greater than the right margin; on the right-hand page, the

_____ margin is greater than the _____ margin.

_ _ _ _ _ _ _ _ _ _ _ _ _ _ _ _

right, left

20. Paragraph <u>headings</u> are an important device of format, because they help the reader to recognize new subjects and to see that certain material is subordinate to a larger subject. The heading identifying the largest subject is called a <u>primary</u> heading, the next smaller subject subordinate to the primary heading is called a <u>secondary heading</u>, and so on.

Look at the headings below in Figure 3-1, Sheet 1.

3-2 BASIC ELEMENTS OF STYLE

3-3 <u>Format</u>

The primary heading is "3-2 BASIC ELEMENTS OF STYLE." The

next lower order of heading, "3-3 Format," is a _____

heading.

— — — — — — — — — — — — — — —

secondary

21. Look at the primary and secondary headings in Figure 3-1. (There
are some tertiary, or third-order, headings, too, but ignore them
for the moment.) How is the form of the primary headings different

from the form of the secondary headings? _____

_____

— — — — — — — — — — — — — — —

The primary headings are in all capitals, while the secondary headings are written with an initial capital letter only (upper and lower
case) and underscored.

22. In a given document, all headings of the same level of importance
should be written in the same form. The "Summary of Style" in
Figure 3-1 has two primary headings. Write them in the space
below exactly as they appear in the figure.

— — — — — — — — — — — — — — —

3-1 DEFINITION OF STYLE
3-2 BASIC ELEMENTS OF STYLE

23. Write the secondary headings under "3-2 BASIC ELEMENTS OF
STYLE," exactly as they appear in the figure.

— — — — — — — — — — — — — — —

3-3   Format
3-4   Language
3-10 Punctuation

24. The heading "3-5 <u>Capitalization</u>" is a tertiary, or third-order, heading. How is it different from the heading numbered 3-4?

_ _ _ _ _ _ _ _ _ _ _ _ _ _ _

It is followed by a period and run-in text (or equivalent answer).

25. How many third-order headings occur under "3-4 <u>Language</u>"?

_ _ _ _ _ _ _ _ _ _ _ _ _ _ _

Five

26. How many third-order headings occur under "3-10 <u>Punctuation</u>"?

_ _ _ _ _ _ _ _ _ _ _ _ _ _ _

Four

27. In most technical documents, the paragraph headings are accompanied by numbers for easier reference. One standard format is to relate the paragraph numbers to the chapter in which they appear. The numbers should all begin with 1 in Chapter 1, 2 in Chapter 2, and so on, and should be followed by -1, -2, and so on in sequence throughout the chapter. Below are the first four headings in Figure 3-1.

    3-1 DEFINITION OF STYLE

    3-2 BASIC ELEMENTS OF STYLE

    3-3 <u>Format</u>

    3-4 <u>Language</u>

Write the next secondary heading that appears in the figure.

_ _ _ _ _ _ _ _ _ _ _ _ _ _ _

3-10 <u>Punctuation</u>

28. Here are some paragraph headings, written in lower case letters only, with paragraph numbers indicated and the headings labeled as primary or secondary.

        4-1 fruits   (primary)
        4-2 apples   (secondary)
        4-3 peaches   (secondary)
        4-4 vegetables (primary)
        4-5 peas   (secondary)
        4-6 carrots   (secondary)

Write the headings below, using the format we have established for primary and secondary headings.

- - - - - - - - - - - - - - -

4-1 FRUITS
4-2 Apples
4-3 Peaches
4-4 VEGETABLES
4-5 Peas
4-6 Carrots

29. Two orders of headings are usually not enough for longer documents. Secondary headings might, in turn, require tertiary headings. Let us assume that we will deal with some subordinate subjects under the secondary heading "Language." The first two subjects are "Capitalization" and "Abbreviation." One form used for tertiary headings is a device called run-in text. These headings are shown on the next page with just enough text to show how they look in print.

3-5 <u>Language</u>

Sometimes no text is required under a secondary (or a primary) heading. If there is text, it is arranged like this.

3-6 <u>Capitalization.</u> Proper names are, of course, capitalized, and so are derivatives of those proper names.

3-7 <u>Abbreviation.</u> The extent to which terms are abbreviated in text is largely a matter of taste, and is often

The next subject under the secondary heading "Language" might be "Spelling." Show this as a third-order heading, adding some of your own writing to indicate run-in text.

_ _ _ _ _ _ _ _ _ _ _ _ _ _ _

3-8 <u>Spelling.</u> Your own words go here as run-in text.

30. There are many variations in format for third-order headings. Two of them are shown below.

3-8 <u>Spelling</u>--Run-in text starts here.

3-8 <u>Spelling.</u>- Run-in text starts here.

If your company publications department has facilities for bold or italic type faces, your latitude in choosing the form of paragraph headings is of course greatly increased.

Even fourth-order headings are not uncommon. Fortunately, there are also ways to handle these. One way is to type the heading exactly as if it were a third-order heading, but without the underscoring.

3-8 <u>Spelling.</u> Run-in text starts here.

A disadvantage of this format for the fourth-order heading is fairly obvious. What is it? _____

_ _ _ _ _ _ _ _ _ _ _ _ _ _ _

The heading does not clearly stand out from the text. (Despite what I regard as a disadvantage, many people use this format for the fourth-order heading. It does, after all, have a paragraph number.)

31. Sometimes fourth-order headings are handled by means of <u>floating heads</u>. An example of this is shown below.

3-5 <u>Secondary Heading</u>

3-6 <u>Third-Order Heading</u>. Note that this heading has both a paragraph number and run-in text.

<u>Fourth-Order Heading</u>. This is called a floating head because there is no paragraph number. Material under a floating head is often regarded as so subordinate that a paragraph number is unnecessary.

The following samples of paragraph headings are not necessarily in descending order. Place a check mark beside the fourth-order heading.

2-4 <u>Lubrication of the Motor-Generator</u>

5-2 SPECIAL TOOLS AND TEST EQUIPMENT

3-8 <u>Theory of Operation</u>

<u>Control Circuit</u>. Refer to Table I for a list of schematic symbols used in this section.

4-6 <u>Troubleshooting</u>. Most common malfunctions are indicated by indicator lights, which are coded according to commonly

— — — — — — — — — — — — — — —

<u>Control Circuit</u>.

32. If you need to go beyond fourth-order headings, you should consider reorganizing your material. Even so, you might not like either of the methods so far described for your fourth-order headings. There is another possibility. Here is our primary heading again.

3-1 DEFINITION OF STYLE

Is there anything you can do to this heading to change its appearance, thereby leaving all capitals as a secondary heading? There is, and you can do it with your pencil. Try it.

3-1 DEFINITION OF STYLE

— — — — — — — — — — — — — — —

3-1 <u>DEFINITION OF STYLE</u>

33. Using our original format, here are two consecutive paragraph headings.

> 3-2 BASIC ELEMENTS OF STYLE

> 3-3 Format

Write the two headings below, using our new format.

- - - - - - - - - - - - - - -

3-2 BASIC ELEMENTS OF STYLE
3-3 FORMAT

34. According to the new format, then, if the primary heading is all capitals underscored, the highest order heading that has run-in text

is the _____ heading.
(third-order/fourth-order)

- - - - - - - - - - - - - - -

fourth-order

35. Instead of varying the written form of the headings, a decimal system for ordering headings is sometimes used (and even at times required). In this system, each lower order heading requires an additional decimal point, as the examples show.

> 3.1   Definition of Style

> 3.2   The Three Basic Elements of Style

> 3.3   Mastering the Elements of Style

> 3.3.1 Format

> 3.3.2 Language

Under the secondary heading "3.3.2 Language," the first third-order heading is "Capitalization." Use the decimal system to write this heading.

- - - - - - - - - - - - - -

3.3.2.1 Capitalization

Note: Although many people consider the decimal system unwiel because of the large extensions of numbers, it can be useful in particular circumstances. The exact form of paragraph headings in the decimal system is quite varied. One might, in addition to the decimal numbering, indicate the order by all capitals, initial capitals underscored, run-in text, etc. The important thing about any syste of ordering paragraph headings is that the format be consistent.

36. The next subject after "3.3.2 Language" and "3.3.2.1 Capitalization" is "Abbreviation." Write this heading in the decimal format.

— — — — — — — — — — — — — — —

3.3.2.2 Abbreviation

37. Arrange the following topics, which are deliberately disorganized, as primary, secondary, and tertiary headings, using the exact format illustrated in Figure 3-1. Assume the material is part of a Chapter 4. Include some run-in text wherever a heading requires it. There is more than one correct order, but only one correct form for each heading.

    diagnosis of common measles (rubeola)
    common measles (rubeola)
    childhood diseases
    treatment of mumps
    diagnosis of mumps
    mumps
    treatment of common measles (rubeola)

— — — — — — — — — — — — — —

There are several correct arrangements, depending on the order in which you list the diseases. Here is one correct arrangement.

4-1 CHILDHOOD DISEASES

4-2 Common Measles (Rubeola)

4-3 Diagnosis of Common Measles (Rubeola). Your run-in text goes here.

4-4 Treatment of Common Measles (Rubeola). Your run-in text goes here.

4-5 Mumps

4-6 Diagnosis of Mumps. Your run-in text goes here.

4-7 Treatment of Mumps. Your run-in text goes here.

38. Indentation refers to the number of spaces from the left margin at which a paragraph begins. The normal indentation is five spaces, although some other spacing might be used. Some documents have ten-space indentation, and some start each paragraph flush left (no spacing). All style guides require some method of distinguishing between paragraphs. (If there is no physical distinction, there is no paragraph.) If you are using a flush-left style (no indentation),

how would you separate paragraphs? _____

_____

– – – – – – – – – – – – – – – –

Use extra line spacing between paragraphs.

39. The methods of pagination, the numbering of pages, are widely variable. If the pages are printed on one side only, the page number is generally centered at the bottom of each page. If the document has back-to-back printing (each page printed on both sides), the page number goes to the outside; that is, on the left side of a left-hand page and on the right side of a right-hand page. The book you are now reading is printed back to back and has the page numbers to the outside at the top. Technical documents in industry are more likely to have the page numbers at the bottom. One very strict rule followed by almost all publications using back-to-back printing is that right-hand pages have odd numbers, and left-hand pages have even numbers.

Without looking at the page itself, state whether page 51 is a

left-hand or a right-hand page. _____

– – – – – – – – – – – – – – – –

right–hand

40. If the document is large enough to be divided into chapters, the pagination is generally related to the chapter. The third page in Chapter 3, for example, would be numbered 3-3. There are two good
reasons for this. Technical documents are changed from time to
time, and the use of sequential numbers within chapters minimizes
the retyping required if material is added or deleted. The other
reason is that the chapter is readily identified without finding the
first page of the chapter.

If the page number is 4-5, that page is the _____ page

of the _____ chapter.

– – – – – – – – – – – – – – – –

fifth page of the fourth chapter

41. Since <u>listings</u> are quite common in technical documents, it is important to understand how this detail of format is generally handled.
Compare the two methods below of listing items in text.

<u>Example 1</u>

The three main causes of malfunctions are fuses,
tubes, and relays.

<u>Example 2</u>

The three main causes of malfunctions are:
a. Fuses
b. Tubes
c. Relays

Which method of listing (Example 1 or Example 2) more clearly

stresses the three main causes of malfunctions? _____

– – – – – – – – – – – – – – – –

Example 2
Note: The stress given by the "a, b, c" listing may not be
necessary. That decision is up to the writer.

42. You might wonder why the listing was labeled "a, b, c" rather than
"1, 2, 3." Numerical listing is equally clear; however, alphabetical
listing is the more general practice. Sometimes there are <u>subordi-
nate</u> <u>listings</u>. These generally follow the form shown on the next
page.

   a. Primary listing

      1. Secondary listing

         (a) Third-order listing (tertiary)

            (1) Fourth-order listing (quaternary)

Further subordinate listings are rare. If they are required, you might consider reorganizing your material. If you have to use them, you would probably go to:

            a) Fifth-order listing

               1) Sixth-order listing.

Study the indentation of the subordinate listings in the examples shown. What rule should be followed in indenting subordinate listings?

— — — — — — — — — — — — — — — — —

Each subordinate letter or numeral is flush with the text of the next higher order listing.

43. The examples shown in frame 42 are to illustrate the <u>labeling</u> of the listings. You should never encounter the exact sequence of listings shown in the examples because of a basic rule about listings: There should never be an "a" without a "b," a "1" without a "2," etc. If you find yourself using a "1" but not a "2," the "1" listing should be incorporated in the preceding text. Look at the following examples.

Example 1

   a. If the "Status" indicator glows red:
      1. Turn POWER A switch to STANDBY.
      2. Turn POWER B switch to OFF.
   b. If the "Status" indicator glows green:
      1. Turn MAIN CONSOLE switch to OPERATE.
   c. Turn FIRING CIRCUIT switch to FIRE.

Example 2

   a. If the "Status" indicator glows red:
      1. Turn POWER A switch to STANDBY.
      2. Turn POWER B switch to OFF.
   b. If the "Status" indicator glows green, turn MAIN CONSOLE switch to OPERATE.
   c. Turn FIRING CIRCUIT switch to FIRE.

Of Example 1 and Example 2 on the preceding page, which is the preferable method of listing? _____

– – – – – – – – – – – – – – – –

Example 2. (Compare "b" in the two examples.)

44. If the sequence of the items in a listing is not important, <u>bullets</u> may be used instead of letters or numerals. Notice the difference between Example 1 and Example 2 below.

    Example 1

    g. Perform the preliminary check as follows:
- Turn CALIBRATE switch to CALIB. The indicator light should glow green.
- Turn BATT/CART switch to BATT. The indicator light should glow red.
- Turn BATT/CART switch to CART. The indicator light should glow yellow.

    Example 2

    g. Copies of the work order should be sent to:
- Director of Operations
- Project Manager
- Division Headquarters

Which of the examples illustrates an acceptable use of bullets?

_____

– – – – – – – – – – – – – – – –

Example 2. (The order is important in Example 1, but not in Example 2.)

45. The steps of the preliminary check in Example 1 of frame 44 are performed in sequence. Would they be labeled "a, b, c," "1, 2, 3," or "(1), (2), (3)"? _____

– – – – – – – – – – – – – – – –

"1, 2, 3"

46. There are other important matters of format to be considered in any writing job. These include the numbering and titles of tables, graphs, and charts, figure numbers and captions, the sequence and arrangement of front matter (such as the title page, contents pages, and abstract), and a variety of other details.

Figure 3-2 illustrates a typical contents page. In this case, only section headings and primary paragraph headings are listed. In a very long and complex document, lower order headings might also be shown. You should make your decision about this by considering the <u>minimum</u> information necessary to help the reader find the material he wants.

Note that the foreword is found on page ii and a program summary on page iii. The contents page, as illustrated, is page iv. The title page accounts for page i, but it is not actually numbered. Lists of illustrations and tables, if applicable, would follow the listing of text matter and would appear on pages v, vi, etc.

How is the pagination of front matter different from the pagination of the body of a document? _____

- - - - - - - - - - - - - - - -

The page numbers are shown in lower-case Roman numerals.

It is pointless to provide general guidelines for details of format such as are encountered in the front matter, because they are extremely variable. The main point about any detail of format is to find out how to handle it by examining similar documents or by consulting a style guide, and then to be sure you are consistent in format throughout the manuscript.

Review on Format

Following are some review questions on the section you have just read. Test your understanding of format before you continue to the next section, on language. The answers are located on page 54.

(a) In establishing margins, more space is generally left at the

_____ than at the _____, and

the side margins are generally _____.

(b) Insert numbers in the parentheses below to indicate the order of the paragraph headings, starting with "1" for the primary heading.

( ) Control Room Equipment

( ) SYSTEM ANALYSIS

( ) Interlock System. Run-in text.

( ) CONTROL SYSTEM

NASA CR-1723

CONTENTS

Section		Page
	FOREWORD	ii
	PROGRAM SUMMARY	iii
1	INTRODUCTION AND OBJECTIVES	1-1
2	BACKGROUND	2-1
	2.1 Low Density Polybenzimidazole Composites	2-1
	2.2 Compositions	2-4
	2.3 Polybenzimidazole-Carbon Cloth Laminates	2-9
3	BILLETS AND CYLINDERS	3-1
	3.1 Component Material Studies	3-1
	3.2 Billet Preparation and Properties	3-15
	3.3 Cylinders	3-52
4	LAMINATES	4-1
	4.1 Components	4-1
	4.2 Fabrication and Processing	4-3
	4.3 Laminates Delivered	4-5
	4.4 Laminate Properties and Testing	4-5
5	CONCLUSIONS AND RECOMMENDATIONS	5-1
	5.1 Conclusions	5-1
	5.2 Recommendations	5-4
6	REFERENCES	6-1

iv

Figure 3-2.   Contents page.

(c)   Page 4-17 in a technical manual is most likely to be a page in

Chapter _____ .

(d)   In arranging the following topics as headings, you may need to review
your anatomy. There is one bone in the upper arm, the humerus,
and one bone in the upper leg, the femur. The forearm has two
bones, the ulna and the radius, and the lower leg also has two bones,
the tibia and the fibula. Arrange these topics as primary, secondary,
and tertiary headings, using the format illustrated in Figure 3-1. If
a heading needs run-in text, show it. Assume these topics are included in Chapter 5, entitled "The Skeleton." Use the space below
the list for your headings.

    tibia
    fibula
    arm
    ulna
    leg
    radius
    forearm
    upper leg
    lower leg
    upper arm
    humerus
    femur

(e)   Your technical manual includes many in-text listings of procedure
steps that follow an "a, b, c" format. If you are faced with a situation where you have an "a" listing but no "b" listing, what should

you do? _____

(f)   How are pages of front matter numbered? _____

Answers to Review

(a) More space is generally left at the <u>bottom</u> than at the <u>top</u>, and the side margins are generally <u>equal</u>.

(b) (3) Control Room Equipment
     (2) SYSTEM ANALYSIS
     (4) <u>Interlock System</u>. Run-in text.
     (1) CONTROL SYSTEM

(c) 4

(d) 5-1   ARM
     5-2   <u>Upper Arm</u>
     5-3   <u>Humerus</u>. Run-in text goes here.
     5-4   <u>Forearm</u>
     5-5   <u>Ulna</u>. Run-in text goes here.
     5-6   <u>Radius</u>. Run-in text goes here.
     5-7   LEG
     5-8   <u>Upper Leg</u>
     5-9   <u>Femur</u>. Run-in text goes here.
     5-10 <u>Lower Leg</u>
     5-11 <u>Tibia</u>. Run-in text goes here.
     5-12 <u>Fibula</u>. Run-in text goes here.

   Note: You might have had a different arrangement; for example, you could have listed LEG before ARM, or <u>Radius</u> before <u>Ulna</u>.

(e) Incorporate the single listing in the preceding text.

(f) Lower-case Roman numerals. (The title page accounts for page i but it is not numbered.)

   It might be a good idea to take a break here before you go on to the next section, on language.

Language

Most details of format are easy to master. It is only necessary to find out what the format is for the particular type of document you are writing and then to be consistent in such matters as margins, paragraph headings, indentation, and pagination. The greatest difficulty in style comes in the area of language, which is a very broad term that covers everything related to the way the language appears in print.

Don't be too literal about that word language. As I have explained, it is meant to include everything that is not strictly format, which we have already studied, or punctuation, which we will deal with later in the chapter.

In language, as in the other basic elements of style, this book presents guidelines which reflect fairly standard usage. It is doubtful if any two style guides in the world agree in all particulars, so learn what this book has to offer, and then modify your style as your company policy and your own preferences dictate.

47. Capitalization generally follows well-defined rules, and you are undoubtedly familiar with most of them. If you need to review the rules, the U.S. Government Printing Office Style Manual, or one of the other style guides listed in the bibliography, might be helpful. In this book, we will just touch on a few problem areas.
    Compare the following examples of direct quotations.

    "You can't really mean that," he said. "Where is your evidence?"

    "The only important consideration," she observed, "is the welfare of your family."

When portions of a single quoted sentence are interrupted by an expression such as "he said," the first word of the second portion is not capitalized. Look at the examples below.

    "Stop right there," he said. "That statement is obviously false."

    "How can you be sure," he asked, "That you know what is best for all of us?"

Which of these two sentences is correctly capitalized?

_____

- - - - - - - - - - - - - - - -

The first sentence. (The second sentence is an interrupted single sentence, and the first word of the second portion, "that," should not be capitalized.)

48. Certain words are sometimes used as titles and sometimes merely as common nouns. Such words are capitalized only when they are used as titles. Compare these three examples.

> I want you to meet Dan Weber, Mother.
>
> Have you met my mother, Dan?
>
> Have you met Mother, Dan?

In the first example, "Mother" is being addressed by name—or title (the rule is the same)—so the word is capitalized. In the second example, the mother is neither being addressed nor referred to by name. She is merely identified by family relationship. Thus, "mother" is not capitalized. In the third example, "Mother" is not being addressed, but she is referred to by name (or title), so the word is capitalized.

Now underline any word in the sentence below that you feel should be capitalized.

I think the woman with judge wainwright is his mother.

− − − − − − − − − − − − − − −

Judge Wainwright. (Do not capitalize "mother" in this case.)

49. Underline each word in this sentence that you feel should be capitalized.

Don't worry, mother; the judge is fair.

− − − − − − − − − − − − − − −

Mother. (Do not capitalize "judge" in this case.)

50. Now try one more.

Did you catch any fish on your vacation, judge?

− − − − − − − − − − − − − − −

Judge. "Judge" in this case is used as a name or title.

Note: Not every case is so simple. A woman might refer to her husband as "Henry" in private and as "the Judge" to others. (Logic would require "the" to be capitalized also, but in practice it is not.)

51. For a little more practice, underline all words in the following examples that should be capitalized but are not.

(a) She was an unusually pretty miss.

(b) He had an early appointment with miss Barrett.

(c) The judge was precisely three minutes late, as usual.

(d) The rulings of judge Wainwright were rarely reversed.

(e) Pardon me, miss.

(f) Good morning, judge.

(g) He deferred to chairman Smith on the point.

(h) The committee suddenly found itself without a chairman.

(i) The ship was under the command of captain Grady.

(j) The captain of a ship at sea has nearly absolute authority.

- - - - - - - - - - - - - - - -

(b) Miss; (d) Judge; (e) Miss (A title, even when no name follows, should be capitalized.); (f) Judge; (g) Chairman; (i) Captain.

52. The first word of a title is capitalized regardless of its length. But how about other small words? Study these examples.

"Arsenic and Old Lace"

"Exploring Nature with Your Child"

The Man from Monticello

Is the length of the word the only consideration in deciding whether to capitalize? _____

- - - - - - - - - - - - - - -

no

53. The actual consideration is whether the word is a key or principal word. In the examples in frame 52, some three- and four-letter words were capitalized while others were not. The small words that are not capitalized are usually articles, prepositions, and conjunctions. For simplicity, the following titles are written without quotation marks and with no capitals. Draw a line under each word that should be capitalized.

the call of the wild

the fabric of society

sonnets from the portuguese

teaching your child to read

– – – – – – – – – – – – – – – –

The Call of the Wild;   The Fabric of Society;   Sonnets from the
Portuguese;   Teaching Your Child to Read
    Note: "Your" in the last title is perhaps marginal. I think it is
a key word; you may not.

54. Historical eras, epochs, and important events are generally capitalized, but there is some room for individual preference. Look at
these examples as a general guide.

the Reign of Terror	but	the reign of Louis XIV
the Industrial Revolution	but	industrial diamonds
the Golden Age of Pericles	but	a golden glow

In the following passage, underline all words that should be
capitalized.

Any nation that has endured for very long has been subject to
civil strife. Even the cherokee nation, after its forced move
to the oklahoma territory, had two principal divisions that were
sometimes engaged in bloody disputes. Opposing claims to the
throne in england led to the war of the roses, and the united
states saw brother pitted against brother in the civil war, which
some people call the war between the states.

– – – – – – – – – – – – – – – –

Cherokee Nation; Oklahoma Territory; England; War of the Roses;
United States; Civil War; War Between the States
    Note: If you overlooked some of these, don't worry about it,
as long as you understand the principle.

55. The names of compass points—west, south, northeast—are not
capitalized unless a specific region or area is indicated.

Turn west, go three miles, and then head north.

The publishing industry is largely concentrated in the
East.

Underline each compass point that should be capitalized.

The family settled in the east when it immigrated from Germany. Many of the second generation moved south and west. One son established a factory in the midwest; another bought a ranch in the southwest. By the third generation, many members of the family had traveled farther west to California and the northwest.

East; Midwest; Southwest; Northwest
Note: "Midwest" is not a compass point, but the rule for capitalization applies to prefixes associated with compass points.

56. Abbreviations can be a real problem in technical writing because of conflicting usages: Is "AC," "a. c. ," or "ac" the correct abbreviation for alternating current? (All three are used.) Should you write "40 meters," "40 m. ," or "40 m"? Added to this is the confusion about which abbreviations should be capitalized and which should not.

Technical writing is filled with standard abbreviations because it would be far too cumbersome to spell out frequently occurring terms such as amperes, microseconds, watts, milliamperes, British thermal units, and decibels. Every field of specialization has a style guide that is generally followed throughout the field, and in addition, your company might have its own style guide, which modifies the abbreviations of some terms.

Thus, in your own writing you should abbreviate generally used

technical terms according to a specific _____.

----

style guide

57. The exact abbreviation you use for a particular term is not important, as long as it is easily understood and used consistently throughout. There are some other general guidelines about the use of abbreviations, however. The rule followed by many good technical writers is not to abbreviate words which are not technical terms. In other words, you should spell out all non-technical words, except for weights and measures, and even spell out words like "feet," "pounds," and "gallons," if they occur infrequently. Never abbreviate words simply because they are long, such as "approx. " for "approximately," or "calib. " for "calibrate. "

Underline all abbreviations in the following sentences which should be spelled out.

The findings were provided by the Industrial Research Co.
of Chicago, Ill.

The pulse has a rise time of approx. 10 μsec and a peak
voltage of 1.8 MV.

The quality control mgr. requested a complete test of
10 pct. of all units received.

— — — — — — — — — — — — — — —

Company; Illinois; approximately; manager; percent

58. Abbreviations in technical writing are fairly standard and therefore
    clear. Acronyms, on the other hand, apply usually to a special
    project or group, and they might not be familiar enough to be readily
    understood. A familiar acronym for the cathode ray tube is "CRT."
    Not so familiar is "EMP," which means electromagnetic pulse.
    The technical writer does not establish acronyms, except in rare
    cases, but where he uses one, he must explain it immediately;
    that is, the first time it occurs in the document. Afterwards, he
    may use the acronym without explanation. Here is an example of
    how that is done.

    The heart of the television set is the cathode ray tube
    (CRT). The CRT is more commonly called the picture
    tube.

    Following the pattern of the above example, rewrite the passage
    below.

    One of the early civil rights groups was the Committee on Racial
    Equality. CORE was not alone, of course.

    — — — — — — — — — — — — — —

    One of the early civil rights groups was the Committee on Racial
    Equality (CORE). CORE was not alone, of course.

59. Many inconsistencies in style involve numerals. The most compre-
    hensive list of rules for the use of numerals is probably that found
    in the U.S. Government Printing Office Style Manual, and those
    rules are followed in this book.
    Have you ever tried to grasp the date of a movie during the brief
    time the Roman numeral is flashed on the screen? If so, you will
    certainly agree that "1973" is a lot easier to read than "MCMLXXIII."

Arabic numerals are generally preferable to Roman numerals. But old practices die hard, so you often encounter things like "Section VIII" and "Chapter III" in technical documents. In your own writing, use the modern style and call it "Section 8" or "Chapter 3."

In your writing, do you use Arabic or Roman numerals for chapter, section, and paragraph headings? _____

— — — — — — — — — — — — — — — —

I hope you wrote "Arabic."

60. Figures are used for numbers of 10 or more.

    10 rotors   15 horses   27 books

The numbers "one" through "nine" are spelled out, unless the sentence also includes one or more numbers of 10 or more.

He has two sons and three daughters.

But:

She has 5 children and 14 grandchildren.

Correct the following sentence, in which all numbers are spelled out, to apply the rule about the use of numbers.

The assembly requires four round-head bolts, eight capscrews, twelve nuts, and twenty-four washers.

— — — — — — — — — — — — — — — —

The assembly requires 4 round-head bolts, 8 capscrews, 12 nuts, and 24 washers.

Note: If a number begins a sentence, it is spelled out.

61. Units of measurement, time, and quantity* are expressed in figures. Look at the list of examples which begins on the next page.

—————————————

*Examples are excerpted from the U.S. Government Printing Office Style Manual.

Age:
  6 years old
  52 years 10 months 6 days
  a 3-year-old

Clock time:
  4:30 p. m.
  10 o'clock or 10 p. m.
  0025, 2359 (astronomical and military time)

Dates:
  June 1935; June 29, 1935
  March 6 to April 15, 1935
  May, June, and July, 1935 (but June and July 1935)

Degrees of latitude and longitude:
  longitude 77°04'06" E.
  latitude 49°26'14" N.
  35°30'; 35°30' N.

Measurements:
  7 meters
  about 10 yards
  8 by 12 inches
  8- by 12-inch page
  2 feet by 1 foot 8 inches by 1 foot 3 inches
  $1\frac{1}{2}$ miles
  6 acres
  9 bushels
  1 gallon

Percentage:
  12 percent; 0. 5 percent

Proportion:
  1 to 4
  1:62, 500
  1-3-5

Time:
  6 hours 8 minutes 20 seconds (but four centuries; three
      decades; three quarters)
  8 days
  10 years 3 months 29 days
  7 minutes
  1 month

Unit modifiers:

    5-day week
    8-year-old wine
    8-hour day
    10-foot pole
    $\frac{1}{2}$-inch pipe (or 1/2-inch pipe)
    5-foot-wide entrance

Note, however, that although figures (instead of word expressions of numerals) are used for units of measurement, time, and quantity, this does not affect the other rules for numbers.

The boy had two new baseball bats and a 3-year-old catcher's mitt.

The nine directors meet every 6 months.

Circle any spelled-out numbers in the sentence below that should be written as figures.

Only fifteen men in the plant voted for the seven-hour day.

— — — — — — — — — — — — — —

15; 7-hour

62. Circle any numbers written as figures that should be spelled out.

The 4 partners worked together for 3 years.

— — — — — — — — — — — — — —

four. (The use of "3" with a unit of time does not change the basic rule that the numbers one through nine are spelled out when no number in the sentence is 10 or more.)

63. If _____ men can build _____ small cottages in _____ days,
    (eight/8)   (two/2)   (six/6)

can _____ men build a single cottage in _____ days?
    (sixteen/16)   (three/3)

— — — — — — — — — — — — — —

If 8 men can build 2 small cottages in 6 days, can 16 men build a single cottage in 3 days?

    Note: If "16" had not appeared in the sentence, all figures would have been spelled out except for those before "days."

64. The use of <u>symbols</u> is one subject on which authorities are in general agreement. The technical writer should carefully consider the use of the symbols below.

Symbol	Meaning
&	and
#	number, pounds
%	percent
o	degrees
@	at
'	feet, minutes of arc
''	inches, seconds of arc
+	plus, positive
–	minus, negative

There are other symbols, of course, but these are the ones most likely to be misused. As a general rule, symbols may be used in tables, illustrations, and other applications where there is limited space, but they should not be used in text. However, there are occasional exceptions to this rule.

The degree symbol (^{o}) may be used in text when temperature is indicated, but not when it is related to degrees of arc. Look at the sentences below.

The sum of the angles in a triangle is 180°.

The oven temperature should not be allowed to vary more than 20°.

Which of these sentences illustrates a correct use of the degree symbol? _____

– – – – – – – – – – – – – – – –

The second sentence

65. Be careful about the degree symbol with reference to temperature: You may use the symbol when specifying an exact temperature, but not when "degree" is part of a modifier. The examples on the next page illustrate the difference.

Right: The solution was kept at a constant temperature within a tolerance of 5°.

Wrong: The warning light signals a 20° change in ambient temperature.

Right: The warning light signals a 20-degree change in ambient temperature.

Of the following three sentences, which one illustrates an incorrect use of the degree symbol?

(a) Report any temperature change of more than 15°.

(b) Rotate the mechanism 90 degrees to lock it in place.

(c) Readings were taken at 2° intervals.

_ _ _ _ _ _ _ _ _ _ _ _ _ _ _

Sentence c. (Standard usage is ". . . at 2-degree intervals.")

66. Always spell out "percent" in text, although the symbol % is usually used in tables because of the limited space. ("Percent," rather than "per cent," by the way, seems to be the preferred form of this term among technical writers.)

The percent symbol (%) is usually used in _____

but the term is spelled out in _____.

_ _ _ _ _ _ _ _ _ _ _ _ _ _ _

tables (or limited space, etc.); text

67. The ampersand (&) and the "at" symbol (@) have no place in text, although they may be used where space is limited. These symbols in text give the document an amateurish appearance.

The symbol # should not be used in text for either of its principle meanings, "number" or "pounds." For "number," the abbreviation "No." is usually used, and "pounds" is either spelled out or abbreviated "lb."

In the list below, check the symbol whose use is normally permissible in text.

@	° (related to temperature)
#	° (degrees of arc)
&	%

_ _ _ _ _ _ _ _ _ _ _ _ _ _

^{o} (related to temperature)

68. An interesting and logical change has occurred in technical writing over the past several years in referring to temperature. Formerly, temperature was specified as 18° F., 25° C., etc. Then a variation crept in, removing the space between the degree symbol and the abbreviation for the temperature scale: 18°F (no period), 25°C, etc. Somewhere along the line, writers began to realize that a number followed by "F" or "C" always referred to temperature, so the degree symbol was unnecessary. Thus, the indication of temperature is now frequently written without the degree symbol and without the period following "F" or "C"—or "K" (Kelvin): 18 F, 25 C, 670 K.

Write the following sentence again, using the abbreviation instead of spelled-out words. (Note: The old term "Centigrade" has now been replaced by "Celsius.")

The boiling point of water is two hundred and twelve degrees Fahrenheit or one hundred degrees Celsius.

- - - - - - - - - - - - - - - -

The boiling point of water is 212 F or 100 C. (Also correct is 212°F and 100°C.)

69. The symbols + and − have two meanings in technical writing: "plus" and "minus," and "positive" and "negative." When the meaning is "positive" and "negative," the symbols may be used in text if they are written with a quantity.

The output voltage is +250 v.

The reading at Terminal A is −16 v.

The symbols may not be used merely to take the place of the words "positive" and "negative."

Wrong: Connect the jumper between the − terminals.

Right: Connect the jumper between the negative terminals.

Right: The line voltage is +24 v.

Fill in the blanks in the following sentence.

The _____ terminal is at ground, and the _____ terminal
    (-/negative)   (+/positive)

is at a potential of _____.
                       (25 positive volts/+25 v)

– – – – – – – – – – – – – – –

negative; positive; +25 v

70. The symbols + and – are used only in equations, and never as substitutes for the words "plus" and "minus" in text.

      $P = 10(a + d) - c$

      The total capacitance is the sum of the circuit values
      plus stray capacitance.

      Fill in the blanks.

$R_T = R_1$ _____ R_2.   To arrive at the real energy value, you must
      (plus/+)

calculate the theoretical value _____ heat losses.
                           (minus/-)

– – – – – – – – – – – – – – –

+; minus

71. The last pair of symbols to be considered in this chapter are ' and ".
Each symbol has at least two meanings: ' means either "feet" or
"minutes of arc," and " refers to "inches" or "seconds of arc." In
text, the symbols should not be used for linear measurements;
"feet" and "inches" should be either spelled out or abbreviated.
The symbols may be used in text in such expressions as "175°30'14"
West Longitude."
    If you suddenly noted that the degree symbol is used for an angular
measurement, despite what has been said earlier, you are right.
The symbol is used in referring to degrees of latitude or longitude.
(This usage is rare in technical writing, so just note it in passing.)
    On the next page is a sentence in which all terms have been
spelled out. Rewrite the sentence, using appropriate numbers and
symbols.

The shaft is marked with two scribed lines that are precisely eighteen degrees, forty-two minutes, twenty-seven seconds apart.

– – – – – – – – – – – – – –

The shaft is marked with two scribed lines that are precisely 18°42'27" apart.

72. Fill in the blanks in the following sentence.

The test stand is _____ high and has a diameter of
                   (4 feet 3 inches/4'3")

_____.
(18 inches/18")

– – – – – – – – – – – – – –

4 feet 3 inches; 18 inches
    Note: Also acceptable would be 4 ft. 3 in. ; 18 in. Some style guides require no period after the abbreviation unless the abbreviation spells another word. Thus we would have 4 ft 3 in. ; 18 in.

73. Write this passage, correcting all errors in the use of symbols.

The heavy lever is 30' long & is weighted with 20# of counterweights for easy movement through 180° of arc. The lever must be 100% reliable @ all ambient temperatures above 32 degrees f.

– – – – – – – – – – – – – –

The heavy lever is 30 feet long and is weighted with 20 pounds of counterweights for easy movement through 180 degrees of arc. The lever must be 100 percent reliable at all ambient temperatures above 32 F. (It is also correct to write "32°F. ")

74. <u>Compounding</u> of <u>words</u> is a problem to the technical writer because there are no firm rules for deciding whether the compound is to be written as two separate words (broad jump), a hyphenated compound (broad-gauge), or solid (broadcast). It is a matter of evolution. When the words are first linked in a single concept, they are still separate. Then they become connected with a hyphen, and finally they are written as a single word. Even the most knowledgeable writer must look up some compounds from time to time to discover the preferred method of writing them, and the most complete list of such words is in the U.S. Government Printing Office <u>Style</u> <u>Manual</u>. This is reason enough to have that book conveniently at hand.

   The best way to deal with compounds is to:

   (a) learn the rules.

   (b) compound any way you like, as long as you are consistent.

   (c) look up compounds you are not sure of in a style manual such as that published by the U.S. Government Printing Office.

----

c

75. <u>Spelling</u> is a subject that must be noted in developing good style. It is assumed that the technical writer knows how to spell in the general sense, * but there are conventions about preferred spelling in technical writing. These might be imposed by a military specification called out in the contract, the company style guide, or general technical writing usage.

   As a general guideline, technical writers are wise to choose the more modern spelling when there are alternative spellings. The modern spelling is generally more phonetic, shorter, or simpler than the older form of the word.

   A few examples are given on the next page, to indicate the trend toward modernized spelling. The two lists (modern and conventional) are mixed. Circle the more modern forms of the words.

---

*If you wish to improve your spelling, you might refer to <u>Spelling</u> for <u>Adults</u>, another Self-Teaching Guide by the author of this book.

align	aline
ameba	amoeba
ax	axe
catalogue	catalog
gauge	gage
plow	plough
staunch	stanch
theatre	theater

- - - - - - - - - - - - - - - -

aline; ameba; ax; catalog; gage; plow; stanch; theater

Review on Language

Following are some review questions on the section you have just read. Test your understanding of language before you continue to the next section, on punctuation. The answers are given on the next page.

(a) Underline each word that should be capitalized in this sentence.

"if you don't hurry," she said, "you will never get to the office on time."

(b) Underline each word that should be capitalized in this title.

the prince and the pauper

(c) Underline each word that should be capitalized in this passage.

great numbers of settlers from the east had moved west of the mississippi river before the civil war. afterwards, the wave of population moved on to the pacific ocean, developing the area now sometimes called the far west.

(d) Fill in the blanks.

_____ men entered the competition, but only _____
(Thirty/30   (thirteen/13)

finished. Of the _____, _____ needed medical attention.
(thirteen/13) (five/5)

All entered the hazardous race for only _____ trophies.
(three/3)

(e) Rewrite the following passage, correcting all poor usages in abbreviations.

The optics of the Foote Automatic Satellite Tracker can be rotated approx. 180°, but the #3 rotor tends to stick at temperatures above 100 degrees Fahrenheit. Once this problem has been solved by the Research & Development Section, the FAST will approach 99.5% reliability.

(f) Circle the more modern spellings of the following words.

dialogue	dialog
plow	plough
gage	gauge
amoeba	ameba

(g) What "bible" of general style has a list of most compound words?

_____

Answers to Review

(a) "If you don't hurry," she said, "you will never get to the office on time."

(b) The Prince and the Pauper

(c) Great numbers of settlers from the East had moved west of the Mississippi River before the Civil War. Afterwards, the wave of population moved on to the Pacific Ocean, developing the area now sometimes called the Far West.

(d) Thirty men entered the competition, but only 13 finished. Of the 13, 5 needed medical attention. All entered the hazardous race for only three trophies.

(e) The optics of the Foote Automatic Satellite Tracker (FAST) can be rotated approximately 180 degrees, but the No. 3 rotor tends to stick at temperatures above 100 F. Once this problem has been solved by the Research and Development Section, the FAST will approach 99. 5 percent reliability.

(f) dialog; plow; gage; ameba

(g) U.S. Government Printing Office Style Manual

If you plan to stop pretty soon, this would be a good place.

Punctuation

It is assumed that the technical writer knows the general rules of grammar, including <u>punctuation.</u> These rules are violated so frequently, however, that some of the more common misuses should be examined here.

76. In the use of <u>commas,</u> the rules are still becoming simpler with modern usage. If a comma will help the reader to grasp your meaning more easily, use it; otherwise, leave it out. The comma often indicates a pause, but this alone is not a sufficient guide to its use. It may also be a visual aid.

    One of the ways a comma helps understanding is in the case of two or more adjectives in succession. If the last adjective is closely related to the noun, do not destroy this relationship by using a comma before it. For example, if a lawyer is both ethical and conscientious, he is:

    an ethical, conscientious lawyer.

    But suppose you wish to describe a "conscientious objector" who is ethical. Circle the more meaningful expression below.

    an ethical, conscientious objector

    an ethical conscientious objector

    – – – – – – – – – – – – – –

    an ethical conscientious objector

77. Circle the more appropriate expression to describe a technical article that is clearly written.

    a clear, technical article

    a clear technical article

    – – – – – – – – – – – – –

    a clear technical article

78. Insert a comma in the following expression if you feel it belongs there.

    a charming vivacious lady

    – – – – – – – – – – – – – –

a charming, vivacious lady

79. A very common mistake with commas involves <u>restrictive</u> and <u>nonrestrictive clauses</u>. Study the following sentences, which are identical except for the use of commas.

> The boy, who had dropped his ice cream cone, began to cry. (Nonrestrictive clause)

> The boy who had dropped his ice cream cone began to cry. (Restrictive clause)

Which sentence refers to a boy who must be distinguished from one or more other boys? _____

– – – – – – – – – – – – – – – – –

Second sentence. (Only the boy who had dropped his ice cream cone had reason to cry.)

80. Now compare these sentences.

> The woman, who had not worked since her marriage, was suddenly faced with the need to earn a living.

> The woman who had not worked since her marriage was suddenly faced with the need to earn a living.

Which sentence logically refers to one woman who is not being distinguished from other women? _____

– – – – – – – – – – – – – – – – –

First sentence. (In the second sentence, the woman is being distinguished from other women, who had worked since their marriages.)

81. It seems to be no great problem to decide whether the use of commas is appropriate in the last two frames. But technical writing is filled with cases in which one comma is used when there should be two. Here is an example.

> The module which had undergone thorough testing, was selected for use in the assembly.

The clause "which had undergone thorough testing" is merely additional information about the module. Thus, it is nonrestrictive. If you chose to add another comma (rather than delete the existing comma), where would you put the second comma? _____

_____

- - - - - - - - - - - - - - - - -

The module, which . . .

82. Some of the plates referred to in the following passage have been coated and others have not. Punctuate the passage.

The spark-gap device has only two electrodes one called the anode and the other called the cathode in a gas-filled envelope. Both electrodes which must withstand the effects of high voltage are made of plates coated with a special alloy. These plates are very similar to uncoated plates used elsewhere in the assembly. Be careful to select clean plates which have been coated with the alloy.

- - - - - - - - - - - - - - - - -

The spark-gap device has only two electrodes, one called the anode and the other called the cathode, in a gas-filled envelope. Both electrodes, which must withstand the effects of high voltage, are made of plates coated with a special alloy. These plates are very similar to uncoated plates used elsewhere in the assembly. Be careful to select clean plates which have been coated with the alloy.

83. Sometimes the modifying clause is at the end of the sentence, so only one comma, or no comma, is involved, as the examples below show.

The producers made a small fortune on the musical,
which ran for over three years on Broadway.

He refused to waste his money on a play which had
produced only yawns in New Haven.

Place a check mark beside the sentence below which requires a comma.

The crew congratulated their foreman who had just received
a special award.

The plant manager fired the foreman who had walked off the
job in a fit of anger.

- - - - - - - - - - - - - - - - -

The first sentence. (A crew has only one foreman.)

84. Because of the impersonal nature of technical writing, "which" is a much more common subject of clauses than "who." This is convenient, because there is a test you can make to be sure a clause is restrictive. If you can substitute "that" for "which," the clause is restrictive; that is, it is not set apart with commas. This won't usually work unless you have personal knowledge of the material, because almost any sentence will still make sense after the substitution of "that," although the sense might not be what was originally intended. Since "that" in such situations automatically means the clause is restrictive, many writers deliberately use "that" for most restrictive clauses, reserving "which" for nonrestrictive clauses. It's a good idea.

The sentence below has a nonrestrictive clause; that is, the information set off by commas is not essential to the basic meaning of the sentence, although it does explain why the highway was almost hypnotic.

> The highway, which stretched ahead without a dip or turn, was almost hypnotic.

You can't substitute "that" for "which" in the sentence, because there is no intent to distinguish one highway from other highways. The clause merely adds additional information to the essential statement, "The highway was almost hypnotic."

But suppose you do wish to distinguish between highways, as in this sentence.

> The highway which wound through the hills was not only difficult but dangerous.

The implication is that some other highway (which did not wind through hills) was neither difficult nor dangerous. The sentence means exactly the same thing if "that" is substituted for "which."

If the sentence below has a restrictive clause, substitute "that" for "which"; if the clause is nonrestrictive, set it off with commas.

The sports car which was totally unexpected was the youth's most cherished birthday present.

— — — — — — — — — — — — — — —

The sports car, which was totally unexpected, was the youth's most cherished birthday present.

Note: If you don't set off the clause with commas, there is an implication that the youth received another car, which he expected.

85. Combine all the information in the two short sentences below into one longer sentence and punctuate as necessary.

The relay is sensitive to very low current. It has gold-plated contacts.

_ _ _ _ _ _ _ _ _ _ _ _ _ _

The relay, which has gold-plated contacts, is sensitive to very low current.

86. Combine all the information in these three short sentences into one longer sentence and punctuate as necessary.

He chose the car. The car had a bent fender. He chose it because it cost less.

_ _ _ _ _ _ _ _ _ _ _ _ _ _ _

He chose the car which (or that) had a bent fender because it cost less.

87. Now try combining some information into a single sentence that contains both restrictive and nonrestrictive clauses. (Hint: The words "which," "who," and "but" should appear in the final sentence. The facts are not in the correct order.)

The police had to find the man. They couldn't use radio and television broadcasts. The man they were looking for had stolen a vial of deadly virus. Any radio and television broadcasts would alarm the public.

_ _ _ _ _ _ _ _ _ _ _ _ _ _

The police had to find the man who had stolen a vial of deadly virus, (or ;) but they couldn't use radio and television broadcasts, which would alarm the public.

88. The semicolon is a very useful punctuation mark, but a comma is often incorrectly used in its place. Sentences such as those below are often encountered in writing, technical and otherwise. Wrong punctuation is underscored.

> Don't expect him to change his ways, he never will.

> You won't finish these letters today, however, I don't want you to work overtime.

> He was given two weeks' severance pay, that is, pay to ease the financial burden during the search for new employment.

The correct versions of those sentences are shown below.

> Don't expect him to change his ways; he never will.

> You won't finish these letters today; however, I don't want you to work overtime.

> He was given two weeks' severance pay; that is, pay to ease the financial burden during the search for new employment.

As you can see from the examples, a semicolon indicates a more definite separation between thoughts than a comma does. In fact, the two separate thoughts can often be stated in separate sentences, grammatically, but the connection is a little too close for separate sentences. The semicolon is also used when two independent clauses, expressing closely related concepts, are linked with a connective such as "however," "therefore," "nevertheless," "furthermore," "that is," and "for example." In these cases, the connective is preceded by a semicolon and followed by a comma.

The following sentences have identical constructions, but only the first is internally punctuated. Insert the punctuation in the second sentence.

The proposed project is too expensive; furthermore, it is unnecessary.

He felt the task was hopeless nevertheless he had to try.

- - - - - - - - - - - - - - - -

He felt the task was hopeless; nevertheless, he had to try.

89. Insert the internal punctuation in this sentence.

The restaurant is small and hard to find however the food is
superb.

— — — — — — — — — — — — — — — —

The restaurant is small and hard to find; however, the food is
superb.

90. Two other connectives are frequently used by professional people:
i. e. , an abbreviation for "that is, " and e. g. , which means "for
example. " Writers often use "i. e. " when they mean "e. g. "* Here
are examples of correct usage.

The metal must be annealed; i. e. , heat-treated for toughness.

The design called for a very durable metal; e. g. , titanium.

Insert internal punctuation in the following sentence.

Some means must be found to halt the wage-price spiral i. e.
inflation must be controlled.

— — — — — — — — — — — — — — —

Some means must be found to halt the wage-price spiral; i. e. ,
inflation must be controlled.

91. The semicolon is useful for linking two closely related concepts,
particularly when the second lends emphasis to the first or provides
an interesting twist. Here are two examples.

He is forceful, tactful, charming, and ambitious; he is a
politician.

The project manager wasted no time, accepted no excuses,
allowed no interference; he got things done.

Insert internal punctuation in the following sentence.

Don't expect that computer to solve all your problems it won't.

— — — — — — — — — — — — — — — —

Don't expect that computer to solve all your problems; it won't.

---

*If you are confused about the use of "i. e. " and "e. g. ," remember that
"i. e. " introduces an explanation, while "e. g. " introduces an example.

92. Try one more.

My candidate is idealistic intelligent frank and scrupulously honest he will be defeated.

– – – – – – – – – – – – – – – –

My candidate is idealistic, intelligent, frank, and scrupulously honest; he will be defeated.

93. The colon is a signal to the reader to note what follows: a listing, a fuller explanation, or some other closely related material. Many writers incorrectly use a semicolon where a colon is required, as in the following examples.

Most of the atmosphere is composed of two gases; oxygen and nitrogen.

There is no need to inventory small components; nuts, bolts, and washers.

In each case, the correct punctuation mark is the colon. Insert internal punctuation in the following sentence.

There are three primary colors in oil painting red blue and yellow.

– – – – – – – – – – – – – – – –

There are three primary colors in oil painting: red, blue, and yellow.
Note: Such a sentence is easily rearranged to avoid the need for a colon, but some of the emphasis is lost.

94. Very frequently in technical writing the material following the colon is arranged for greater visual impact, as in this example.

Although there is a wide variation in personalities, five stages of intoxication can be identified:
1. Jocose
2. Bellicose
3. Lachrymose
4. Morose
5. Comatose

Rearrange the following sentence for greater visibility of the elements following the colon. Use the space on the next page.

The three great religions with ties to Jerusalem, in order of age, are: Judaism, Christianity, and Islam.

- - - - - - - - - - - - - - - -

The three great religions with ties to Jerusalem, in order of age, are:
1. Judaism
2. Christianity
3. Islam

95. One special case involving the <u>hyphen</u> should be examined. Unit modifiers (combinations of words that together act as adjectives) are sometimes, but not always, hyphenated. Some examples are: double-edged blade, fiery-eyed radical, two-penny nail. There is no problem unless there are two or more unit modifiers with a common second element; for example, one-penny nails and two-penny nails, or 3-inch bolts and 5-inch bolts. To show the use of economy in writing, here are three progressively briefer ways to say the same thing.

  3-inch bolts and 5-inch bolts

  3-inch and 5-inch bolts

  3- and 5-inch bolts

As you can see, repeating the first (but not the second) element of a unit modifier is clear and direct, but be sure the first element includes the hyphen.
  Following the pattern of the above example, rewrite this sentence.

He needed an assortment of 1-foot, 2-foot, and 3-foot sections of pipe.

- - - - - - - - - - - - - - -

He needed an assortment of 1-, 2-, and 3-foot sections of pipe.

96. The hyphen is used in the same way with compound words that are normally written solid. Look at the examples on the next page.

airtight and watertight compartment

air- and watertight compartment

Rewrite the following sentence using the same pattern.

The store offered a selection of calfskin, pigskin, and deerskin wallets.

– – – – – – – – – – – – – – –

The store offered a selection of calf-, pig-, and deerskin wallets.

Review on Punctuation

Following are some review questions on the section you have just read. Test your understanding of punctuation before you continue to the Self-Test for this chapter on style. The answers to the review are located on the next page.

In the following passages, sentences could be structured in a number of ways, all of them correct. Therefore, assume that there are no mistakes in capitalization and the placement of periods. Insert <u>internal</u> punctuation marks only.

(a) Old wornout cliches are dull therefore try to avoid them. Always keep in mind the three basic elements of style format language and punctuation. Your editing which is an important part of writing will almost always improve your original draft.

(b) The writer who is careless of editorial style is sure to produce a substandard document. Few writers are entirely consistent in style therefore the wise writer will systematically search his own work for inconsistencies.

(c) The 3 inch screws are too long but either 1 or 2 inch screws may be used. Be sure they are of some nonferrous metal i.e. they may be made of aluminum or brass but not of steel.

Answers to Review

(a) Old, wornout cliches are dull; therefore, try to avoid them. Always
keep in mind the three basic elements of style: format, language,
and punctuation. Your editing, which is an important part of writing,
will almost always improve your original draft.

(b) The writer who is careless of editorial style is sure to produce a
substandard document. Few writers are entirely consistent in
style; therefore, the wise writer will systematically search his
own work for inconsistencies.

(c) The 3-inch screws are too long, but either 1- or 2-inch screws may
be used. Be sure they are of some nonferrous metal; i.e., they
may be made of aluminum or brass, but not of steel.

SELF-TEST

These questions will test your understanding of Chapter 3.   Answers
are given following the Self-Test.

1.   Rewrite the following passage, correcting any errors or poor usages
in style, including format, language, and punctuation.   (Hint: Use
Figure 3-1 as a guide.)

5-1 POWER PANEL. The power panel has only two controls which
can be manipulated by the operator however there are three adjustment screws for the convenience of technicians. The operator
controls are described in the following paragraphs.

5-2 Power Switch

A single pole single throw toggle switch which is labeled ON
and OFF provides power to the circuit.

Replacement of Power Switch. This toggle switch almost never
requires maintenance. If it must be replaced however refer to
chapter 6 for the detailed replacement procedure.

2.   Complete the paragraph numbering in the decimal system.

3-1 STYLE	3.1 STYLE
3-2 Format	Format
3-3 Language	Language
3-4 Abbreviations. Run-in	Abbreviations. Run-in text.
text goes here.	

3. The Coin Club, which met promptly at _____ p. m.,
                                              (four-thirty/4:30)

    devoted its entire meeting to _____ gold pieces and _____
                                   (five/5)   (twelve/12)
    silver coins.

4. When the pages of a document are printed on both sides, the page

    number usually goes _____.
                        (top center, bottom center, outside, inside)

5. Rewrite the following passage, correcting language and punctuation.

    A 5" test tube is used in the Standard Catalytic Action Test
    therefore measurements must be very precise. The SCAT requires
    25% Miller formula, 70% dist. water, and 5% SCAT compound @
    25 degrees Celsius. Two #6 test probes & a negative six volt power
    source should be available before the procedure is started. The
    alternate test which varies somewhat from the primary procedure
    is available from the Test & Analysis Section.

6. Punctuate the following passage according to the general guidelines
    in this chapter.

    One must not assume that a foster home is the only solution
    it isn't. Johnny Staunton's five year case history is typical however
    generalizations can be misleading. Johnny's parents who are di-
    vorced lost custody of their child while they were still married
    after a thorough investigation by the Social Service Agency Johnny
    found himself in a foster home it was the first of many.

7. Rewrite the following passage according to the general guidelines in this chapter.

The prime contractor, interested but not persuaded, requested supplementary data, i.e., a back-up report on the three and five-foot titanium sections including test data on the electrical effect of the 15° bend radius. At issue were two factors; arcing and line resistance. "It is plain, common sense," the liaison officer remarked, "To be absolutely sure about the side effects."

Answers to Self-Test

If your answers to the test questions do not agree with the ones given below, you may wish to review the chapter. Specific frame references are not given for review because questions are drawn from many parts of the chapter.

1. There are, of course, many details of punctuation that are variable, so don't be concerned as long as you feel your version of the passage is correct. Here is the recommended version.

5-1 POWER PANEL
    The power panel has only two controls which can be manipulated by the operator; however, there are three adjustment screws for the convenience of technicians. The operator controls are described in the following paragraphs.

5-2 Power Switch
    A single-pole, single-throw, toggle switch, which is labeled ON and OFF, provides power to the circuit.

5-3 <u>Replacement of Power Switch</u>. This toggle switch almost never requires maintenance. If it must be replaced, however, refer to Chapter 6 for the detailed replacement procedure.

2.   3.1   STYLE
    3.1.1   <u>Format</u>
    3.1.2   <u>Language</u>
    3.1.2.1 <u>Abbreviations</u>. Run-in text goes here.

3.   The Coin Club, which met promptly at 4:30 p.m., devoted its entire meeting to 5 gold pieces and 12 silver coins.

4.   outside

5.   This is one version; yours might differ in some details.

    A 5-inch test tube is used in the Standard Catalytic Action Test (SCAT); therefore, measurements must be very precise. The SCAT requires 25 percent Miller formula, 70 percent distilled water, and 5 percent SCAT compound at 25 C. Two No. 6 test probes and a -6-volt power source should be available before the procedure is started. The alternate test, which varies somewhat from the primary procedure, is available from the Test and Analysis Section.

6.   Here is the punctuated passage. If your punctuation differs, be sure you know the reason for the difference.

    One must not assume that a foster home is the only solution; it isn't. Johnny Staunton's five-year case history is typical; however, generalizations can be misleading. Johnny's parents, who are divorced, lost custody of their child while they were still married. After a thorough investigation by the Social Service Agency, Johnny found himself in a foster home; it was the first of many.

7.   Here is a suggested version; yours might differ in some details.

    The prime contractor, interested but not persuaded, requested supplementary data; i.e., a backup report on the 3- and 5-foot titanium sections, including test data on the electrical effect of the 15-degree bend radius. At issue were two factors: arcing and line resistance.
    "It is plain common sense," the liaison officer remarked, "to be absolutely sure about the side effects."

CHAPTER FOUR
Technical Review

It is quite possible that this chapter is not for you. If you write only in your specialized field, drawing upon your own knowledge and experience, there is no need to go through the technical review procedure, because you automatically review the accuracy of your information as you work through the material toward the final draft. If that is true of you, you may wish to skim Chapter 4 quickly or even skip it entirely.

Most technical writers in business and industry, however, must draw on the specialized knowledge of others—scientists, engineers, or other experts—in preparing their material. This chapter is short, but it is very important for such writers.

No matter how well written your document is, it fails to the extent that it is less than accurate. Even the most knowledgeable writer must take calculated risks if he is writing from the raw input of someone else. It is easy to change the sense of a sentence while tightening up the phraseology or rearranging an awkward statement for better construction. A good technical review is your best defense against the pitfalls inherent in your interpretation of someone else's information.

When you complete this chapter, you will be able to:

- minimize rewriting required by the technical review;

- arrange a technical review;

- provide review copies for participants in the formal review.

1. A responsible writer would not for a moment think of publishing a technical document without first making sure that it was thoroughly reviewed for technical accuracy. Therefore, the technical review is an important step in preparing material of any significance. *

---

*While this book is concerned only with reviews for technical accuracy, please note that your writing may be subject to other reviews as well. Some of these are policy reviews by management, patent and other legal reviews, and marketing reviews.

The writer might have a number of informal conferences with engineers or other experts from the very beginning of the writing project, but when the writing is complete, the formal technical review is the logical step to insure complete accuracy in the published version of the document. It is the writer's way of asking those persons who are the source of his information, "Have I interpreted your information correctly? Is my presentation complete and accurate? Does it really convey the information it was intended to convey?"

Of course, the writer does not really ask questions in that way. Instead, he provides copies of the completed document to all necessary reviewers, schedules a conference far enough ahead to allow his reviewers to study the material, then conducts a formal review in which the material is gone over page by page while questionable points are discussed and changes and corrections noted.

The actual writing of a technical document is the business of the writer alone, but the technical review is a means to insure

_____.

_ _ _ _ _ _ _ _ _ _ _ _ _ _ _ _ _

accuracy

2. The writer should be confident of his ability to present technical information clearly and accurately, but he should not be overconfident. If he communicates frequently with his technical experts, the formal review will present few surprises. If the writer has not had preliminary, informal checks on his accuracy, he might find a kingsized job of rewriting necessary after the formal review.

Assume you have just finished a fairly complicated circuit description, which is part of a chapter in a maintenance manual. You wrote the description from the notes of a very busy design engineer, and you want the engineer to check the accuracy of your description. Your best procedure is to:

(a) Call the engineer and read your description to him, noting changes and corrections as he mentions them.

(b) Go to his office and go over the description with him.

(c) Give him a copy of the circuit description for him to review and mark at his convenience.

_____

_ _ _ _ _ _ _ _ _ _ _ _ _ _ _ _ _

Procedure (c) is most efficient, least subject to error, and most considerate of a busy engineer. It also saves your time, because you can go on to something else while the engineer reviews and corrects your description.

3. It is important to work closely with your experts. Sometimes a telephone call might be the best way to clarify some detail, or a few minutes of personal conversation with the expert might be well spent. If you do choose to provide the written material itself for the expert's review, a bit of psychology will do no harm: If the material requiring review is presented in fairly small sections, it is more likely to get prompt attention. The expert is encouraged to undertake a small task immediately; he might be tempted to put aside a larger job "until he has more time."

Which of the choices below would the expert be more likely to review immediately?

(a) a complete document

(b) a fairly substantial section, such as a few chapters

(c) a fairly short section, such as a chapter

– – – – – – – – – – – – – – – –

c

Note: Sometimes you cannot submit a small portion, because the reviewer has to see the material in context.

4. You probably have a deadline for completion of your writing project, or at least you have a fair idea when it will be finished. Therefore, to avoid wasting time and delaying the final publication of your document, you have to set a reasonable date for your formal review; that is, you must give sufficient notice to reviewers to insure their attendance. Announce the date in any practical manner—telephone calls, personal visits, or a memorandum—but be sure to get firm commitments of attendance.

If several people are to attend a formal review, and one or two cannot meet at the appointed time, there is no real problem. You can provide review copies for them and meet separately to get their comments. This is not the best way, but it is sometimes unavoidable. If most of the reviewers are unable to attend, you must pick another date.

The formal review is as much for all the reviewers as for yourself. Reviewers need to discuss points with each other, while you merely listen, because each person brings his own perspective to the formal review. The approach, the emphasis on certain matters, and even whether some material should be deleted are all subject to differing opinions that have to be aired until a consensus is achieved.

The date of your formal review should be acceptable to

_____ of your reviewers.
(all/most/some)

— — — — — — — — — — — — — — — —

most

5. Review copies of your document must be made available to the re-
    viewers before the formal review, because they must have time to
    read the document and mark in corrections, changes, questions, or
    comments. The longer or more difficult the document, the longer
    the time that must be allowed for review.

    Let us assume you expect to complete your writing on March 31.
    Two days are required for reproduction of the review copies, and
    you have decided that two weeks are sufficient for the reviewers to
    read and mark your document. Check the date below on which you
    should schedule the formal review.

    April 5

    April 16

    May 1

— — — — — — — — — — — — — — — —

April 16

6. The document should be retyped to incorporate your own editing
    before review copies are reproduced, but corrections on the typing
    or other small editorial changes may be marked in. The point is
    to provide each reviewer with a copy that is easy to read; it need
    not look like a published document.

    It is easy to overlook comments written into review copies, be-
    cause the copies are reproduced with black ink, and many reviewers
    use a black pen or pencil to write in comments. It is a good idea to
    encourage reviewers to use some other color for their comments.
    One way is to include a statement on the cover sheet (which gives
    the date and time of the formal review), requesting the reviewer to
    use any color but black in marking the copy.

    How can you avoid a massive rewrite because of errors discovered

    at the formal review? _____

    _____

— — — — — — — — — — — — — — —

Get preliminary, informal reviews of your writing.

7. After the formal review, you will collect all review copies and compare them with your own copy, which you mark during the review. Parts of your copy can look pretty garbled after changes (and changes to changes) are written in, so you should make sure a few extra review copies are available for your later use. It is a good idea to keep three copies for your own use and perhaps three more copies for unexpected reviewers or to replace lost copies.

Assume you are ready to order review copies of a document for a formal review at which you expect four experts. What is the minimum number of copies you should order? _____

– – – – – – – – – – – – – – – –

10: 4 for reviewers, 3 for yourself, and 3 extras

8. The formal review itself is simple, because the purpose is simple: to make the document as accurate as possible.

The writer is the logical person to preside over the formal review. The meeting itself is actually quite informal, with the only rules being those of simple courtesy.

Since each reviewer has read and marked his review copy in advance, the formal review is merely a process of going through the document, page by page, and resolving any errors. The writer marks in each change, then reads back the sentence or phrase, as modified, to confirm the exact wording of the change.

While the formal review is supposed to be concerned with technical information only, not writing, most experts delight in pointing out grammatical or typographical errors! The writer should not resent this; the most careful writer can make mistakes and overlook typos. Help from any quarter should be welcome.

What is the purpose of the formal review? _____

_____

– – – – – – – – – – – – – – – –

The formal review is intended to insure technical accuracy. It is primarily concerned with the information presented, not the manner of presentation. (Or an equivalent answer.)

9. At the end of the formal review, you should collect all review copies for reference during incorporation of comments. Before the final draft is typed, you must be sure every correction or change written in each reviewer's copy is incorporated or accounted for. If you do not want to make a suggested change, you must discuss it with the reviewer. To ignore a reviewer's comments is to invite anger or hurt feelings and to damage prospects for future cooperation.

Which of the following procedures (any or all may be correct) should you use to incorporate review comments in the final draft?

(a) Write in each change as it is decided during the formal review.

(b) Check each review copy to be sure all changes are accounted for.

(c) Discuss any disagreement about a change with the appropriate reviewer.

──────────

─ ─ ─ ─ ─ ─ ─ ─ ─ ─ ─ ─ ─ ─ ─ ─

You should follow all three procedures.

SELF-TEST

These questions will test your understanding of Chapter 4.   Answers are given on the following page.

1.   What is the main purpose of a technical review, formal or informal?

   _____

2.   How can you best reduce the amount of rewriting because of errors discovered at the formal technical review?

   _____

3.   In deciding the number of copies of your document to be reproduced for the technical review, you should consider:

   (a)   _____

   (b)   _____

   (c)   _____

4.   In fixing a date for the formal review, you need to consider:

   (a)   _____

   (b)   _____

5.   If five reviewers are invited to the formal review, and only four can attend, you should pick another date if this presents no real problem. If it is difficult to set another date, what is your best procedure?

   (a)   Delay the formal review until all can attend, regardless of the length of delay.

   (b)   Go ahead with the formal review, reasoning that four out of five reviewers will insure a sufficient technical review.

   (c)   Go ahead with the review and make a separate appointment to get the comments of the fifth reviewer.

   _____

6. As the writer conducting the formal technical review, you will dis-
    cover that the reviewers:

    (a) have little to say.

    (b) frequently disagree with each other.

    (c) often arrive at the review conference without sufficient prepara-
         tion.

    _____

7. If, during incorporation of review comments, you feel you should
    not make a change, what should you do?

    _____

Answers to Self-Test

If your answers to the test questions do not agree with the ones given
below, review the frames indicated in parentheses after each answer
before you go on to the next chapter.

1. The main purpose of any technical review is to insure technical
    accuracy. (frames 1, 8, and 9)

2. You should submit portions of your document to the appropriate ex-
    perts for their review during the original writing. (frames 2 and 3)

3. (a) your own requirements
    (b) the number of copies to be sent out for review
    (c) extra copies for unforeseen circumstances, such as an unex-
         pected reviewer or a lost copy
    (frame 7)

4. (a) the length of time needed for reviewers to review the document
    (b) the availability of your reviewers at the scheduled time
    (frames 4 and 5)

5. c (frame 4)

6. b. Answers a and c may be true, at least sometimes, but those
    answers are not justified by the material in the chapter. (frames
    4 and 8)

7. Discuss the questionable change with the expert who requested it.
    (frame 9)

CHAPTER FIVE
Production

When you complete this chapter, you will be able to:

- identify the other people involved in producing a technical document;

- identify the specific responsibilities of the technical writer in coordinating his work with other people involved in assembling the complete document.

Writing the material that will eventually appear as text in the printed document is only part of the technical writer's job. Even when there are no illustrations in the document, he still has to have the original writing, or "rough draft," typed one or more times. The typed copy has to be edited, and then the whole thing has to be typed in final form, ready for printing. Usually there are illustrations, which brings the art or photography department (or both) into the act. Finally, the writer will have some contact with the printer even before delivery of the final package for printing, because in most companies the print shop is responsible for a number of things besides printing.

THE PRODUCTION TEAM

The members of the production team vary with the size and organization of the company and even with the size of the publication job, but the team usually includes at least the following people.

Technical Writer. He or she writes the text, decides how the text should be illustrated (photographs, drawings, tables, charts, graphs), and has primary responsibility for the final printed document.

Technical Editor. This is often the writer wearing a different hat, but in larger companies someone else edits the material. The editor is responsible for the technical accuracy and clarity of both text and illustrations. It is the editor's job to see that the document is complete and error-free and to prepare it for printing.

Technical Typist. The manuscript is typed as received from the writer, providing the editor with a clean copy. After editing, the final copy is typed for reproduction as the printed document. The callouts (text matter on illustrations) are also typed and become part of the finished artwork. The technical typist, whose job is sometimes underrated by writers and editors, is a key member (often the key member) of the production team.

Technical Illustrator. The art department (graphic arts) ranges from a separate department with its own department head to a single artist in one corner of the publications department. The artist is responsible for everything from simple line drawings to highly professional airbrush renderings in color. An example of a line drawing with callouts (text matter) is shown below.

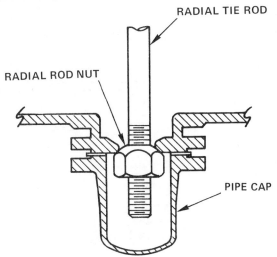

Photographer. A required photograph might be in the files, but the photographer often has to shoot new pictures at the request of the writer. Large companies, and many small ones, will probably have a photo lab.

Printer. The print shop is often called the reproduction department, because this department is involved in production of the document long before final printing. Oversize artwork has to be reduced to fit the available space, screened negatives have to be prepared for the printing of photographs, and tables, charts, and graphs may have to be reduced for pasteup in the "camera-ready" package. Printing is sometimes sent to an outside vendor, but the writer in industry is more likely to find that printing is done "in house."

1. The original text of a technical document is prepared by the

    _____.

    — — — — — — — — — — — — — — — —

    technical writer

2. A clean copy of the writer's text is prepared by the _____

    _____.

    — — — — — — — — — — — — — — —

    technical typist

3. The _____ corrects errors and
    omissions in the text, makes changes to improve clarity and to
    insure technical accuracy, and otherwise controls the final form of
    the text.

    — — — — — — — — — — — — — — —

    technical editor.   (The writer may do this job himself.)

4. The _____ prepares line drawings,
    schematics, and other types of illustrations that are not photographs.

    — — — — — — — — — — — — — — —

    artist or technical illustrator

5. Photographs used in the document are provided by the

    _____.

    — — — — — — — — — — — — — — — —

    photographer, photo lab, or photography department

6. After the text is edited, the final copy used for printing is prepared
    by the _____.

    — — — — — — — — — — — — — — —

    technical typist

7. Reproduction of the final document is the responsibility of the

    _____.

    — — — — — — — — — — — — — — — —

    printer or print shop

8. The print shop is sometimes called the _____

    _____.

    – – – – – – – – – – – – – –

    reproduction department. (The jargon for this is "repro.")

9. Reduction of a piece of oversized artwork is the responsibility of the

    _____.

    – – – – – – – – – – – – –

    print shop or reproduction department

10. List the main people involved in the preparation of a technical
    document.

    – – – – – – – – – – – – – –

    technical writer, technical editor, technical typist, technical illus-
    trator, photographer, printer

THE PRODUCTION PROCESS

The entire procedure that results in a finished technical document is
called "production" because it is not merely written; it is <u>produced</u>. To
see how this is done, let's follow a small document from start to finish.

  We'll assume the writer has to prepare a short description of a
power supply for use with a computer made by another company. The
writer works for a company that has a contract to furnish the power
supply to the customer; that is, the other company. The description of
the power supply is needed by design engineers and other technical people
employed by the customer.

  The writer's work begins when he gets some kind of request for the
document. This could be a formal work order or an informal instruction
from his supervisor. For simplicity, we will leave out details such as
the charge number (the account to which time is charged) and other administrative matters.

  After conferring with the engineer who has designed the power supply,
the writer decides that two illustrations will be sufficient—a schematic
diagram of the electrical circuit and a photograph of the power supply.

11. The writer can't wait until the writing is finished to begin arrange-
     ments for the illustrations, because this would be an unnecessary
     waste of time. During the writing, he might decide he needs more
     illustrations, but at least he wants to get the illustrations started.
     The engineer has given him a pencil sketch as a basis for the sche-
     matic diagram of the electrical circuit. He takes the sketch to the

     _____.

     _ _ _ _ _ _ _ _ _ _ _ _ _ _ _ _

     artist. (From now on, we'll dispense with the term "technical
     illustrator.")

12. The power supply is a new design, so there is no existing photograph

     for the writer to use. He contacts the _____
     to arrange for a picture.

     _ _ _ _ _ _ _ _ _ _ _ _ _ _ _ _

     photo lab or photographer

13. The schematic diagram includes a transformer, resistors, capaci-
     tors, and other components that have to be labeled on the finished
     drawing. Depending on the organization of the publications depart-
     ment, the preparation of the callouts (text matter) on the drawing
     might be arranged for by the artist, by the writer, or by someone
     else. In any case, the callouts, to be pasted on the drawing, are

     prepared by the _____.

     _ _ _ _ _ _ _ _ _ _ _ _ _ _ _ _

     technical typist

14. If the writer knows how to type, his rough draft is probably written
     on his own typewriter. Assuming that changes in the text will not
     be extensive enough to change the page count, the writer knows that
     there will be three text pages in the final document. The format he
     is using requires each illustration to be on a separate page. The
     document will have a title page, but no other front matter, such as
     a table of contents. The pages of the final document will be printed
     on one side only. What is the total page count of the final document?

     _____

     _ _ _ _ _ _ _ _ _ _ _ _ _ _ _

     Six pages: a title page, three pages of text, and one page each for
     a photograph and a schematic diagram.

15. The writer's typed text pages, the finished schematic diagram, and the photograph have to be checked for completeness and accuracy, and changes may have to be made before the document is ready for

printing.   The text and illustrations now go to the _____

_____.

– – – – – – – – – – – – – – – –

technical editor.   (If the technical writer does this job himself, he picks up the photograph and drawing when they are ready.)

16. The editor finds that one electrical symbol on the schematic diagram is not as shown on the pencil sketch.   There are also some changes to

be made in the text.   He confers with the _____
about the electrical symbol and gives the marked text to the

_____.

– – – – – – – – – – – – – – – –

artist; technical typist

17. The schematic diagram had to be drawn oversize.   After the problem about the electrical symbol is resolved, the editor takes the line art

to the _____ to have a reduced print made.

– – – – – – – – – – – – – – – –

reproduction department or print shop

18. After conferring with the publications supervisor, the editor* decides that 20 copies of the document should go to the customer, 10 should be distributed to engineering people inside the home company, and 2 copies will be filed in the publications department.   In addition, the writer will receive 1 copy, and the technical library will get 2

copies.   Therefore, the _____ will be

instructed to print _____ copies of the document.

– – – – – – – – – – – – – – – –

---

*If the editor is different from the writer, he is usually senior in the production process.   In such cases, the writer normally does not worry about distribution.

printer; 35.   Actually, the print order will probably be for 40 copies, in case there are additional requests for the document.   It's a lot cheaper to run five extra copies than to run a new printing.

Other people are involved in preparation of the final document.   For example, various experts will have a chance to check the work for technical accuracy during the technical review, which was described in Chapter 4.   But these operations, discussed elsewhere in this book, are not really part of the production process.

The step-by-step operation we have examined varies quite a bit with the type of document and the nature of the company, but the production steps are basically the same for any kind of technical publication.

SELF-TEST

These questions will test your understanding of Chapter 5.   Answers are provided following the Self-Test.

1.   List the main people involved in the production of a technical document.

2.   Who prepares the original text?   _____

3.   Who arranges for illustrations?   _____

4.   The two people who actually prepare the illustrations are the

_____ and the _____.

5.   Who makes changes in text matter and illustrations?

_____

6.   Sometimes the technical writer acts as his own _____.

7.   Who provides reduced prints of illustrations?   _____

8.   Who is the last person involved in the production process?

_____

Answers to Self-Test

If your answers to the test questions do not agree with the ones given below, review the frames indicated in parentheses after each answer before you go on to the next chapter.

1.   technical writer, technical editor, technical typist, artist, photographer, printer (reproduction department).   (frames 1—7)

2.   technical writer   (frame 1)

3.   technical writer   (frame 11)

4. artist; photographer. (If you included the preparation of callouts for the line art, you have to add the technical typist.) (frames 11 and 12)

5. technical editor (frame 15)

6. editor (frame 3)

7. reproduction department (print shop) (frame 17)

8. the printer. (Distribution of the document is not part of the production process. This necessary step is discussed in Chapter 6.) (frame 7)

CHAPTER SIX

Preparing the
Printer's Package

This chapter contains useful information whether you are employed as a
technical writer or sometimes write on technical subjects in connection
with some other position. In either case, you are writing for publication, and the preparation of the printer's package—that is, the finished
material from which plates are made for printing—is a necessary step
in the production process, which was described in Chapter 5.

When you have finished this chapter, you will be able to:

- arrange for the preparation of page negatives;

- identify the kinds of errors to look for in checking the final text;

- assemble the text and illustrations in their proper order in a
  "printer's package."

1. The technical writer is often responsible for the entire job of assembling the document into a "printer's package." Even if he is not, he
   can do a better job if he knows something about the printing process.
   There are two general methods of printing: <u>letterpress</u> ("hot type")
   and <u>offset</u> ("cold type"). Letterpress printing is still very much in
   use for a great many applications, but almost all industrial publications are produced by offset printing, which is also called "lithography."

   What is the most common method of printing in industry?

   _____

   _ _ _ _ _ _ _ _ _ _ _ _ _ _ _

   offset or lithography

2. The <u>plate</u>, which is put on the printing press and produces the final
   printed page, may be of paper, plastic, or metal. We need not be
   concerned with just how the plate is made; we need only know that
   sometimes the plate is made directly from the original typed

material or the original artwork, and sometimes it is made from a negative.

A plate is made from a negative if:

there is a photograph on that page, or

oversize artwork must be reduced, and the print shop does not have the facilities for reduction of positives, or

the artwork contains very small details, fine lines, or some other characteristic that requires the use of a line negative in producing the plate.

All the plates used in printing a document could be made from negatives, but this is unnecessarily expensive, so most text pages are printed from plates made from the original typed copy rather than from negatives.

A plate is most likely to be made from an original rather than from a negative when:

(a) there is a photograph on the page.

(b) artwork on the page has fine lines or small details.

(c) the page has only text.

_____

_ _ _ _ _ _ _ _ _ _ _ _ _ _ _ _

c

3. It is important to understand the difference between a <u>line</u> <u>negative</u> and a <u>screened</u> <u>negative</u>. If everything on the page is either solid black or white (no shades of gray), the negative used in making a plate is a line negative. If you hold a line negative up to the light, you will see that everything on the negative is either transparent (black on the printed page) or opaque (white on the printed page). Since there are no shades of gray, the production of the line negative is relatively simple.

A line negative "shot" from a printed page will show text as

_____.

(transparent/opaque)

_ _ _ _ _ _ _ _ _ _ _ _ _ _ _

transparent

4.   A printed page that includes shades of gray must be produced from

a _____ negative.

– – – – – – – – – – – – – – – –

screened. (A line negative produces only pure black and white.)

5.   In the printing trade a photograph is called a <u>halftone.</u> This means
that the printed page will have more than black and white contrast;
it will also have shades of gray. Halftone may also describe illustrations other than photographs which include tones that are not pure
black. (Wash, for example, is a technique that produces gray areas.)
For all practical purposes, however, halftone generally means a
photograph.

To faithfully reproduce the shades of gray in a photograph, the
printer must shoot the photograph with a screen. The screen con-
verts the art to a series of dots. Smaller, less dense dots will
appear in the lighter areas of the halftone; larger, more dense dots
will appear in the darker parts. These dots, which appear as
transparent in the halftone negative, will print black on the positively
printed page. In other words, the dots simulate a continuous tone
photograph. You can see how these dots work by examining a halftone in a newspaper where the paper and quality of the halftone make
it obvious to the naked eye.

From the writer's point of view, the only difficulty with a screened
negative is that the printer cannot "paint out" blemishes with opaquing
fluid as he can on a line negative. (Opaquing is a technique routinely
used with line negatives, because it is almost impossible to produce
a negative with large opaque areas and no blemishes, scratches, or
light spots.) If there are blemishes on a screened negative, it must
be shot again, and time is wasted.

A negative on which the image is produced from patterns of dots

is a _____ negative.
         (line/screened)

– – – – – – – – – – – – – –

screened

6.   A plate used to print a halftone must be made from a _____
negative.

– – – – – – – – – – – – –

screened

7.   Illustrations are of two general types: line art and halftones. Line art is generally artwork drawn with pen and ink. It is often over-size, requiring later reduction, either because it is easier for the artist to draw the illustration oversize, or because callouts must be added to the artwork, and there must be space to place the callouts, which are normally typed.

Photographs, too, usually need to be reduced, simply because a standard size for photographs is 8 by 10 inches, while the standard image area (area on the page exclusive of margins, page number, and document number) is about $6\frac{1}{2}$ by $8\frac{1}{2}$ inches.

Sometimes a photograph or a piece of artwork must be enlarged. Decisions about the size of illustrations and the preparation of nega-tives are made earlier in the production process, discussed in Chapter 5. We have to consider the negatives again here because they are part of the printer's package, and the writer must control and account for each of them.

The two main types of illustration are _____

and _____ .

– – – – – – – – – – – – – – – – –

line art (or drawings) and halftones (usually photographs)

8.   Although photographs can be reduced (or enlarged) and converted to halftone negatives early in the production process, they are not placed in position until the type is set and the final page is made up and shot in negative form. The addition of line negative to halftone negative is called stripping in. Line drawings, without tone, can be stripped onto the typed page and shot with the page. Figure captions and page numbers are usually added to the page in the final typing. They are, therefore, shot with the page for a one-piece line negative.

Why are page numbers added or stripped in only in the final

typing? _____

– – – – – – – – – – – – – – – – –

Because page numbers are assigned during final typing.

9.   Work on your document is going on at different places during the production process. Negatives are being prepared in the print shop or reproduction department, artwork is being prepared in the art department, and your text is being typed by the technical typist. (You have, of course, kept track of all this activity!) Your job in preparing the printer's package is to retrieve all this material and assemble it.

The text is the simplest part of the process to describe, but it involves the most painstaking work, because most of the errors in a document are in text. Therefore, it must receive the careful attention of a technical editor (let us assume that this person is you) who corrects the final text and returns it to the technical typist for corrections before the printer's package is assembled.

Your final check of the typed manuscript is mechanical but important. After final typing, when the text pages are <u>camera-ready</u> (that is, ready for plate-making), you must check each page for proper page number, document number (if there is one), margins, and arrangement of text.

In checking the page numbers, you must be careful to allow a page number for each illustration page. Although illustrations are sometimes integrated with text, most technical documents have illustrations on separate pages. An illustration usually follows the first text page on which there is a reference to it.

In your document of several chapters, the first text reference to

Figure 4-7 is on page 4-15. The next <u>text</u> page is page _____.

_ _ _ _ _ _ _ _ _ _ _ _ _ _ _ _ _

4-17. (Figure 4-7 is on page 4-16.)

10. If your document is to have pages printed on one side only, the document number usually goes above the text on the right-hand side of the page. If printing is to be back to back (each page printed on both sides), the document number goes above the text and to the outside. Remember that in back-to-back printing, all right-hand pages have odd numbers, while left-hand pages have even numbers.

Assume that in checking the document numbers of a document to be printed back to back, you notice that two consecutive pages, 3-13 and 3-14, have the document number located on the left-hand side of

the page. Page _____ has the document number incorrectly
                  (3-13/3-14)
located.

_ _ _ _ _ _ _ _ _ _ _ _ _ _ _ _ _

3-13. The outside margin of a right-hand (odd-numbered) page is on the right. A left-hand location for the document number on this page is incorrect.

11. There are standard rules of format that the technical typist (or any other typist) should know but might overlook. Therefore, you have to check for such errors as incorrect hyphenation of divided words, leaving a colon at the bottom of a page, or allowing a paragraph heading to stand at the bottom of a page without following text.

In checking the typed document, what two kinds of errors should you check for? _____

- - - - - - - - - - - - - - -

typographical errors and errors of format

12. When the text is in final typing, some procedure must be followed to be sure all illustrations, both line art and halftones, fall on the appropriate pages. One procedure is to type all the line copy—document number, page number, and caption—in the correct locations on the page. A line negative might be prepared from this page and the illustration later stripped in, or the printer might be given instructions for later stripping in the line copy on illustration negatives. In either case, insertion of these almost empty pages is a good way to avoid omission of an illustration page.

An alternative procedure is merely to instruct the typist to insert the illustration pages from the draft into the final document without typing.

Anything that works is all right, but the important thing is to be sure that _____ pages are accounted for

and inserted in the proper _____.

- - - - - - - - - - - - - - -

illustration; order (or sequence)

13. The preparation of front matter, in the case of documents long enough to warrant it, is another task that must wait until after the final typing of text. The front matter varies with the type of document, but it always includes at least the title page and the table of contents. It sometimes includes an abstract, a proprietary notice, or an acknowledgments page.

The title page and abstract, if there is one, could be typed along with the rest of the text, but the table of contents includes page numbers, and these are not known until the text has gone through final typing and the last edit.

The check of the table of contents, aside from reading for ordinary typographical errors, includes two principal tasks: to check page numbers against the text, and to check paragraph headings for correct style and consistency in wording with the same paragraph headings in the text.

The two main things to check in the table of contents are

_____ and _____.

- - - - - - - - - - - - - - -

paragraph headings, page numbers

14. The <u>printer's dummy</u> is a reference for the printer to be sure each page is accounted for. It is also a guide to text pages and pages to be printed from negatives. Here is a portion of a printer's dummy (also called a "printer's map").

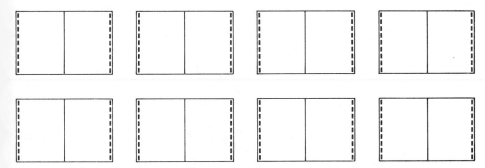

Notice that the binding is shown on the outside. This is confusing at first, but there is a practical reason for it. Since any document starts on a right–hand page and ends on a left–hand page (even if the page is blank), it makes sense to start the printer's dummy the same way.

If your document is to be printed on one side only, you merely draw vertical lines through all the left–hand pages (which, remember, are shown in the right–hand position). If the document is to be printed back to back, you use all pages, or perhaps "X" out a single page to be left blank.

The same printer's dummy is shown again below, but this time the pages have been marked. (It is a help to the printer to identify new chapters, but text pages are generally left blank except for the page numbers. You needn't bother to locate the page numbers properly; bottom center is all right.) Illustration pages are, of course, identified, both as to the type of illustration and the figure number. Since our portion of the printer's dummy has 16 pages, we will map out a document of that length.

Chap 1	Fig 1-1 Line Art		Fig 1-2 HT			Fig 1-3 Line Art	
1-1	1-2	1-3	1-4	1-5	1-6	1-7	1-8

Chap 2		Chap 3	Fig 3-1 HT				
2-1	2-2	3-1	3-2	3-3	3-4	3-5	

Is the document on the preceding page printed one side only or back to back? _____

_ _ _ _ _ _ _ _ _ _ _ _ _ _ _ _

back to back

15. How many screened negatives (for halftones) are in the printer's package? _____ What are their figure numbers?

_____

_ _ _ _ _ _ _ _ _ _ _ _ _ _ _ _

Two; Figures 1-2 and 3-1

16. Two figures are line art—not line negatives. What are their figure numbers and page numbers? _____

_ _ _ _ _ _ _ _ _ _ _ _ _ _ _ _

Figure 1-1, page 1-2; Figure 1-3, page 1-7

17. Is the last page of the document blank or printed? _____

_ _ _ _ _ _ _ _ _ _ _ _ _ _ _ _

The "X" on this page means that it is blank.

18. You are preparing a printer's dummy for a document which is to be printed on one side only. The first eight pages in Chapter 4 of your document are listed below.

    4-1 Text
    4-2 Figure 4-1, a line drawing
    4-3 Text
    4-4 Text
    4-5 Figure 4-2, a photograph
    4-6 Figure 4-3, a line negative
    4-7 Text
    4-8 Text

Fill in the pages of the printer's dummy at the top of the next page.

Your printer's dummy should look something like this.

A few other details must be arranged when the complete printer's package is submitted for printing. The printer has to know the number of copies, the kind of paper, and the kind of binding, for example. The responsibility for giving this information to the printer might be the writer's or someone else's, but someone must make these decisions. If you don't know how these things are decided in your company, you will learn the first time you have to supervise the printing of a document.

SELF–TEST

These questions will test your understanding of Chapter 6. Answers are given on the following page.

1. The plate used to print a page can be made from the original page of the typed manuscript or from a _____.

2. If the printed material must be reproduced in shades of gray, rather than solid black and white, the plate must be made from a

   _____ negative.

3. A screened negative has an image composed of patterns of dots, while a _____ negative does not.

4. Most halftones used in technical documents are _____.

5. A negative has been shot for an illustration page early in the production process, but the page number cannot be stripped in until final typing of the document. Why? _____

6. The document number for page 5–18, in a document printed back to back, is located in the upper right-hand corner of the page. What is wrong with the location of the document number? _____

   _____

7. What important part of the document, basides page numbers, is prepared only after final typing of the document is completed?

   _____

8. The two main things to check in the table of contents are

   _____ and _____.

9. You are preparing a printer's dummy for a document which is to be printed on one side only. The first eight pages of Chapter 3 of your document are listed on the next page. Look at the list, then fill in the pages of the printer's dummy which follows.

3-1   Text
3-2   Figure 3-1, a photograph
3-3   Text
3-4   Figure 3-2, line art
3-5   Text
3-6   Figure 3-3, line negative
3-7   Text
3-8   Text

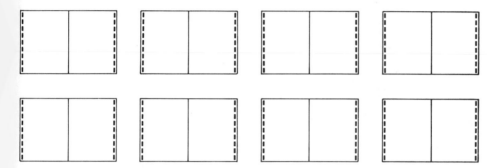

Answers to Self-Test

If your answers to the test questions do not agree with the ones given below, review the frames indicated in parentheses after each answer before you go on to the next chapter.

1.   negative   (frame 2)

2.   screened   (frames 2—7)

3.   line   (frames 2 and 3)

4.   photographs   (frame 5)

5.   The exact page numbers are unknown until final typing.   (frame 9)

6.   Page 5-18 is a left-hand page, so the document number should go in the upper left-hand corner of the page.   (Left-hand pages have even page numbers.)   (frame 10)

7.   Table of Contents   (frame 13)

8.   paragraph headings and page numbers   (frame 13)

9. Your printer's dummy should look something like this.

(frames 14–18)

PART TWO
Effective Writing

Part One was concerned with some of the routine procedures that are a necessary part of preparing technical publications, but it had little to do with <u>writing</u> itself.

Part Two deals with the actual use of the language in conveying information, which is what technical writing is all about.

Part Two will help you to:

- avoid the pitfalls of grammar in technical writing;

- edit your own work or that of other writers;

- write functional sentences that communicate your thoughts clearly and accurately;

- choose words and phrases that will add clarity and impact to your writing.

CHAPTER SEVEN

Grammar

The purpose of this chapter is not to teach you basic grammar. You might be weak on some points, but you probably are not interested in a course on the basics of English grammar. English grammar, however, has pitfalls, even for the experienced writer. This chapter will give you a review of some of the finer (or perhaps cloudier) points in the grammar of technical writing.

When you finish this chapter, you will be able to:

- apply modern rules for the agreement of subject and verb;

- make sure your pronouns and their antecedents agree;

- avoid ambiguous reference of pronouns;

- use the appropriate modifier with a gerund.

1. You know, of course, that a verb must agree with its subject in person and number. If the subject is a singular noun, the verb is singular. Mistakes occur, however, when the form of the noun is not the same as its sense. The writer must consider the actual meaning of his subject, not just the structure of the words. A collective noun deserves some thought about its sense, whether it is singular or plural.

    The noun "data" confuses many writers. It is borrowed from Latin, and in form it is clearly the plural of "datum," which means "something given." But as often happens with Latin words, the singular form is rarely encountered. Thus, the writer who is too narrowly concerned with the structure of the word, rather than its real meaning, is likely to regard it as always plural and to violently disagree with anyone who wants to assign a singular verb to it.

    In modern English usage, "data" has two separate meanings. It can mean "bits of information," but it can also mean "a body of information." Compare the two sentences on the next page.

The data are fed into the computer by means of punched cards.

The raw data has to be corrected to remove anomalies.

In the first sentence, the sense of "data" is "bits of information." In the second, the whole collection of data is examined for anomalies, so it is more accurate to think of the raw data as a unit.

Choose the preferable pronoun in the sentence below.

An independent group examined the data and decided that _____

proved the hypothesis.   (it/they)

- - - - - - - - - - - - - - - -

it. (The <u>body</u> of data was examined, so "data" can mean "information.")

2. Some data _____ erroneous, but the overall conclusion was

valid.   (was/were)

- - - - - - - - - - - - - - - -

were. (But this is marginal; it depends on how you thought of the data. If you thought of data as a body of information, "was" would be correct.)

Note: As you can see, one can argue for singular or plural in many cases. The important thing is to be sure all related words are of the same number. Don't write, "These data are startling. It proves . . ."

3. If a collective noun can be regarded as a unit, the verb is singular. If, on the other hand, the members of the collective noun seem to be acting as individuals, the verb is plural. Select the appropriate verbs in these sentences.

(a) The committee _____ praised by the chairman.
                  (was/were)

(b) The committee _____ of various opinions.
                  (was/were)

- - - - - - - - - - - - - - - -

(a) was; (b) were

4. Now try two more.

(a) The majority _____ in a democracy.
      (rule/rules)

(b) The majority _____ farmers, hunters, and fishermen.
      (is/are)

- - - - - - - - - - - - - - - -

(a) rules; (b) are

5. Sometimes the <u>form</u> of the noun is clearly plural, but the <u>sense</u> is just as clearly singular.

Forty pounds is the overseas weight limit.

The life and work of Goethe is the subject of the biography.

Select the appropriate verbs in these sentences.

(a) The last 10 miles _____ the hardest part of the hike.
      (was/were)

(b) More than 15,000 votes _____ not counted.
      (was/were)

(c) Twenty million votes _____ hardly a mandate.
      (is/are)

- - - - - - - - - - - - - - - -

(a) was; (b) were; (c) is

6. The number of the predicate nominative (underlined in these exampl) has no effect on the number of the verb.

The pressing problem is higher <u>prices.</u>

The most boring part of the program is the <u>speeches.</u>

Select the appropriate verbs in these sentences.

(a) The immediate concern of the police _____ riots.
      (was/were)

(b) The topic of the final lecture _____ diseases.
      (was/were)

- - - - - - - - - - - - - - - -

(a) was; (b) was

7. Sometimes a subject has two or more parts that differ in number or person. This often happens with the pairs "either . . . or" and "neither . . . nor." In such cases, the verb agrees with the nearer part of the subject.

> Neither he nor his friends were invited.
>
> Neither his friends nor he was invited.
>
> Either you or I am mistaken.
>
> Either I or you are mistaken.

Select the appropriate verbs in these sentences.

(a) Either he or you _____ to stay at home.
                            (has/have)

(b) Neither her friends nor she _____ to blame.
                                    (was/were)

(c) Either he or the twins _____ lying.
                              (is/are)

- - - - - - - - - - - - - - -

(a) have; (b) was; (c) are

8. Often, in technical writing, a qualifying phrase or clause falls between the subject and the verb, leading the unwary writer to be influenced by a nearer noun that is not the subject of the sentence. In each of the following sentences, the verb has the wrong number.

> The presence of unsanitary conditions make contamination inevitable.
>
> Distractions from any source during the experiment makes concentration difficult.

You should check the verb by looking only at the simple subject and its corresponding verb.

> Presence <u>makes</u>.
>
> Distractions <u>make</u>.

Select the appropriate verbs in the sentences on the next page.

(a) The process by which unlimited needs are ranked in priority in comparison with limited resources _____ been thoroughly (has/have) studied.

(b) When living conditions resulting from poor crops and the shortag of food _____ below the subsistence level, starvation results (falls/fall)

— — — — — — — — — — — — — — — —

(a) has; (b) fall

9. A pronoun always agrees in person, number, and gender with its antecedent.

A <u>mother</u> instinctively tries to protect <u>her</u> children.

<u>People</u> usually try to rationalize <u>their</u> failures.

Select the appropriate pronouns in these sentences.

(a) All members of each group must do _____ share. (its/their)

(b) Every employee in the higher echelons of management must set a good example for _____ subordinates. (his/their)

— — — — — — — — — — — — — — —

(a) their; (b) his

10. The <u>case</u> of a pronoun (nominative, objective, genitive) depends on its function. If the pronoun is the subject of a sentence, the case is nominative.

<u>He</u> had no interest in economics.

<u>They</u> agreed on most things but differed about politics.

If the pronoun receives the action, its case is objective.

Economics did not interest <u>him.</u>

They agreed on most things, but politics divided <u>them.</u>

If the pronoun shows possession, the case is genitive.

His interest in economics was nonexistent.

Their only difference of opinion lay in politics.

Most people automatically select the correct pronouns in sentences similar to these examples, but things get a bit confused when the pronoun functions in a clause or some other sentence fragment. And most of the errors involve forms of "who."

Whom did you select for the promotion? (You did select whom?)

You may choose whomever you wish. (Choose whomever.)

The task will be assigned to whoever volunteers for it. (Whoever volunteers.)

In the first two examples, the choice of case is fairly simple. The third, however, requires a little more thought. The object of "to" is a clause (whoever volunteers for it), and "whoever," not "whomever," is the subject of the clause.
Select the appropriate pronouns in these sentences.

(a) The trophy will go to _____ is best.
(whoever/whomever)

(b) He was determined to fire _____ he found to be
(whoever/whomever)
responsible.

– – – – – – – – – – – – – – – –

(a) whoever; (b) whomever

11. Select the appropriate pronouns in these sentences.

(a) _____ did you reward for the suggestion?
(Who/Whom)

(b) _____ do you feel is the best candidate for the honor?
(Who/Whom)

– – – – – – – – – – – – – – – –

(a) Whom; (b) Who

12. The antecedent of a pronoun is the noun to which the pronoun relates. The antecedent of a pronoun such as "who" or "that" determines whether a verb following that pronoun should be singular or plural. Look at the examples on the next page.

He is a man who never worries about money.   ("Who"
refers to "man.")

He is one of those rare men who never worry about money.
("Who" refers to "men," not to "one.")

It was one of those days that try one's patience.   ("That"
refers to "days," not to "one.")

Select the appropriate verbs in these sentences.

(a) She was one of those people who _____ to love everyone.
     (seem/seems)

(b) It was one of those experiences that _____ a vital
     lesson.   (teach/teaches)

(a) seem.   ("People who seem"; not "one who seems.")
(b) teach.   ("Experiences that teach"; not "one that teaches.")

13. Pronouns such as "anybody," "anyone," "everyone," and "neither"
     imply situations in which more than one person is involved; thus, it
     is easy to think of the group rather than the singular pronoun in
     choosing a related pronoun. Here are two examples of this common
     error.

     Wrong: Everyone must look after their own arrangements.

     Wrong: Neither of them knew their contracts had been
             canceled.

These sentences should be written in the following manner.

     Right: Everyone must look after his own arrangements.

     Right: Neither of them knew his contract had been
               canceled.

Select the correct pronouns in the following sentences.

(a) Everyone had to make _____ before breakfast.
                          (his bed/their beds)

(b) Anyone late for work will have _____ pay docked.
                                    (his/their)

(a) his bed; (b) his

14. Many sentences are ambiguous because the personal pronoun can refer to more than one antecedent.

> Mary told her mother that she needed a new coat. (Who needs the new coat?)

Some writers avoid the ambiguity with a sentence that is still awkward.

> Mary told her mother that she (Mary) needed a new coat.

The parenthetical "Mary" is an admission that the sentence is otherwise unclear. A better solution is to use a direct quotation.

> Mary told her mother, "I need a new coat."

Rewrite the following sentence to remove the ambiguity.

Bennett told Carson that he would have to find another job.
(Note: Carson will be job-hunting.)

_____

- - - - - - - - - - - - - - - -

Bennett told Carson, "You will have to find another job."
    Note: If you revised the sentence, "Bennett told Carson to find another job," you changed the sense of the sentence. Bennett did not tell him to find another job; he told Carson, rather obliquely, that he had lost his current job.

15. A <u>gerund</u> is a verb form ending in -ing that is used as a noun. A common error in writing is the incorrect use of a pronoun in the objective case with a gerund. Since the pronoun must modify the gerund, the possessive case is correct. The gerunds are underlined in these examples.

> Wrong: The supervisor objected to us <u>coming</u> to work late.

> Right: The supervisor objected to our <u>coming</u> to work late.

Select the appropriate pronoun in the following sentences.

(a) His colleagues resented _____ winning the appointment as Department Chief.
    (him/his)

(b) The Division Manager approved _____ taking a leave of absence.
    (him/his)

- - - - - - - - - - - - - - - -

(a) his; (b) his

16. A more subtle error occurs when a noun rather than a pronoun is used with a gerund.

> Wrong: The boss disliked his secretary shopping during her lunch hour. (He didn't dislike his secretary; he disliked her shopping.)

> Right: The boss disliked his secretary's shopping during her lunch hour.

Rewrite the following sentence.

The company was disturbed by the union striking for higher pay.

The company was disturbed by the union's striking for higher pay. (The company would not be disturbed by the union itself, as long as it didn't strike.)

SELF-TEST

These questions will test your understanding of Chapter 7. Answers are given on the following page.

Correct all grammatical errors in the following sentences. Space is allowed for your notations.

1. Although the jury were carefully instructed by the judge, who obviously thought the defendant was innocent, neither the defense lawyers nor the accused man were certain that the outcome would be an acquittal.

2. The jury was in almost violent disagreement from the beginning of deliberations, and everyone was determined to argue their views at great length.

3. Forty minutes were the minimum time between ballots; and after three days, most of the jurors deeply resented the lone holdout and sharply criticized him arguing for conviction.

4. The cause of the lone juror's arguments were two pieces of circumstantial evidence presented by an unreliable witness.

5. The jury foreman sarcastically observed, "The majority rule, even here," to which the holdout retorted, "Everyone has a right to defend their own opinion."

6. The foreman proceeded to give the holdout a stern lecture, and a woman juror told him he was being unreasonable.

7. "If any one of you raises their voice again, I'll never change my vote," the angry holdout yelled.

8. "Who do you want to punish, the foreman or the defendant?" an elderly juror asked.

9. "Neither you nor anyone else have the right to insult me," the lone juror said. "The force of all your arguments mean nothing to me. I resent you trying to pressure me."

10. The holdout juror was one of those men who seems to love argument for its own sake, because on the next ballot, he voted for acquittal.

11. As the defendant, at last a free man, shook hands with his attorneys, he said, "I'm glad everyone has a right to their day in court; I'm guilty as hell!"

Answers to Self-Test

If your answers to the test questions do not agree with the ones given below, you may wish to review the chapter. Specific frame references are not given for review because questions are drawn from many parts of the chapter. Corrections to grammatical errors are underscored.

1. Although the jury was carefully instructed by the judge, who obviously thought the defendant was innocent, neither the defense lawyers nor the accused man was certain that the outcome would be an acquittal.

2. The jury were in almost violent disagreement from the beginning of deliberations, and everyone was determined to argue his views at great length.

3. Forty minutes <u>was</u> the minimum time between ballots; and after
    three days, most of the jurors deeply resented the lone holdout and
    sharply criticized <u>his</u> arguing for conviction.

4. The cause of the lone juror's arguments <u>was</u> two pieces of circum-
    stantial evidence presented by an unreliable witness.

5. The jury foreman sarcastically observed, "The majority <u>rules</u>, even
    here," to which the holdout retorted, "Everyone has a right to defend
    <u>his</u> own opinion."

6. It is unclear from this sentence <u>whom</u> the woman juror accused of
    being unreasonable. Here are two possible versions of the corrected
    sentence.

    The foreman proceeded to give the holdout a stern lecture, and a
    woman juror told <u>the foreman</u>, <u>"You</u> <u>are</u> <u>being</u> <u>unreasonable."</u>

    The foreman proceeded to give the holdout a stern lecture, and a
    woman juror told <u>the holdout</u>, <u>"You</u> <u>are</u> <u>being</u> <u>unreasonable."</u>

7. "If any one of you raises <u>his</u> voice again, I'll never change my vote,"
    the angry holdout yelled.

8. "<u>Whom</u> do you want to punish, the foreman or the defendant?" an el-
    derly juror said.

9. "Neither you nor anyone else <u>has</u> the right to insult me," the lone
    juror said. "The force of all your arguments <u>means</u> nothing to me.
    I resent <u>your</u> trying to pressure me."

10. The holdout juror was one of those men who <u>seem</u> to love argument
    for its own sake, because on the next ballot, he voted for acquittal.

11. As the defendant, at last a free man, shook hands with his attorney,
    he said, "I'm glad everyone has a right to <u>his</u> day in court; I'm
    guilty as hell!"

CHAPTER EIGHT
Editing

Sometimes the writer is his own editor, in which case he thinks of his self-editing as rewriting. More commonly, his work is edited by someone else. (This is often true even of a technical professional writing in his own field, unless it is a private article for a professional journal.) In either case, he is a better writer if he is also a good editor.

When you complete this chapter, you will be able to:

- use the standard editing symbols;

- work with the technical typist in preparing camera-ready copy;

- recognize the limitations an editor should observe in working with another writer's material.

EDITING SYMBOLS

Editing symbols (also called "proofreader's marks") are the means by which the editor communicates with his typist in ordering corrections or changes to the typescript. The wise editor will make sure the typist understands his symbols, both to save time and effort and to avoid ruffled feelings.

The symbols taught in this book are standard, but there may be local variations. Just be sure your typist knows what you mean. (If there is doubt, you can always write a note in the margin.)

1. A capital letter is <u>upper case</u> and a small letter is <u>lower case</u>. In the sentence below, note the symbols that are used to change the "case" of a letter.

   Edited: you should have a good background in American History.

   Typed: You should have a good background in American history.

Edit this sentence. Mark the sentence with the symbols, then write the sentence as it would be typed.

Mr. jones resigned his Position at harvard.

Edited: Mr. jones resigned his Position at harvard.
Typed: Mr. Jones resigned his position at Harvard.

2. The symbol for lower case is _____ .

/

3. The symbol for upper case is _____ .

≡

4. "A" means:

   (a) make the "A" lower case.

   (b) delete the "A."

a

5. Examine this edited sentence.

   Several words have been misused.

   The symbol # means _____ .

leave a space

6. Examine this edited sentence.

   Several words have been misused.

   The symbol ͻ means _____ .

close up, or no space

7. To indicate a space, use the symbol _____.

— — — — — — — — — — — — — — —

♯

8. To close up a space, use the symbol _____.

— — — — — — — — — — — — — — —

⌣

9. Complete this chart.

Meaning	Symbol
Lower case	
Upper case	
Space	
Close up	

— — — — — — — — — — — — —

Lower case: /
Upper case: ≡
Space: ♯
Close up: ⌣

10. Edit this passage.

The italian city of Florenceis a Favorite city of artists,
partly be cause it bears the stamp of michelangelo. One
of his most famous sculptures, the statue of david, is
there.

— — — — — — — — — — — — — —

The italian city of Florence is a favorite city of artists, partly
be cause it bears the stamp of michelangelo. One of his most
famous sculptures, the statue of david, is there.
    Note: The space symbol can also be placed differently:
Florence is.

11. You often need to insert something new into the text. The symbol that shows where the insertion goes is called a <u>caret</u> and is used like this:

The caret is used ^to show the addition of something.

Insert the word "is" in the appropriate location.

His success due to hard work.

— — — — — — — — — — — — — — —

His success ^is due to hard work.

12. The delete symbol is used like this.

He insisted that ~~that~~ the meter had been calibrated.

He insisted that the meter had been calibrated.

When something is deleted, a space is left. Sometimes you may want to make it clear that you do not want a space left; in this case you can combine the delete and close up symbols, as in the sentence below.

The second division was performed on January 2, 1974.

Edit this sentence.

We asked for your opinion opinion on the mattter.

— — — — — — — — — — — — — — —

We asked for your opinion ~~opinion~~ on the matter.

13. Edit this sentence.

Arizona is locatedd in the United States America.

— — — — — — — — — — — — — — —

Arizona is located in the United States ^of America.

14. Edit this sentence, substituting "because of" for "due to" and making any other changes that seem necessary.

Due to the heavy traffic on the nimitz free way, the

guestspeaker was 20 minutes late.

— — — — — — — — — — — — — — —

Because of
~~Due to~~ the heavy traffic on the nimitz free way, the guest speaker
was 20 minutes late.

15. A common typographical error is the transposition of letters or
words. The symbol used to deal with this is quite clear.

recieve   on way the to work

Edit this sentence.

All phases the of system have bene thoruoghly tested.

- - - - - - - - - - - - - - - -

All phases the of system have bene thoruoghly tested.

16. Sometimes material must be moved to a different position in the
sentence. Here is how this is done.

Circle the text to a new location to be moved and draw an
arrow to the required position. Also use a to indicate the
point of insertion.   Caret

Edit this sentence to begin with "Answers."

On the following page answers are given.

- - - - - - - - - - - - - - - -

On the following page answers are given.
Note: Remember that you must account for any changes in
capitalization and punctuation which occur when you rearrange
sentences. In this sentence, "On" is marked for lower case and
"answers" is marked for upper case.

17. The symbol for beginning a paragraph is shown in this example.

This is the final sentence of a paragraph. The new
paragraph should start with this sentence.

Edit this passage, starting a new paragraph with the word
"American." Remember to catch the other errors, too.

It is clear, then, that injustcie to minorities is not new.

American history is with filled examplesof the mis treat-

ment of the Indains.

- - - - - - - - - - - - - - - -

It is clear, then, that injustice to minorities is not new. ⁀American history is (with filled) examples of the mis‿treatment of the Indians.

18. Two different symbols are commonly used to indicate "no paragraph." They are shown in the examples below.

the market analysis.
no ¶ New York presented a unique problem.

the market analysis. ⌣
⌐New York presented a unique problem.

For simplicity, we will use the symbol no ¶ .
Edit this passage, assuming that the second sentence does not start a new paragraph.

Lubricate the bearing with DC-212 lubricnt, which is made

by the dow corning company.

If dc-212 is not available, an equivalent may used.

– – – – – – – – – – – – – – –

Lubricate the bearing with DC-212 lubri$\overset{a}{\wedge}$cnt, which is made by the dow corning company.
no ¶ If dc-212 is not available, an equivalent may $\overset{be}{\wedge}$used.

19. The comma, semicolon, and colon are merely inserted in text as required. The period and hyphen, however, require special treatment to avoid misunderstandings.

A period goes at the end of this sentence⊙

You should hyphenate "right=hand."

The double line is used to indicate a hyphen because a single line might be overlooked. A period is encircled for the same reason.
Edit this passage.

Limes oranges, and other citrus fruits are important

suorces of Vitamin c   Many people take ascorbic acid

tablets, however, vitamin rich fruits are preferable to

synthetics from the drug store.

– – – – – – – – – – – – – – –

Limes, oranges, and other citrus fruits are important sources of Vitamin c⊙ Many people take ascorbic acid tablets; however, vitamin=rich fruits are preferable to synthetics from the drug store.

20. A routine editing chore is to indicate that certain abbreviations should be spelled out. One convention is to circle the abbreviation to be spelled out, but the more common symbol is shown below.

The shortest section of pipe is 2 in. long.

Edit this sentence.

The American Mining Co. was first listed on the N. Y. Stock

exchange on Jan. 21.

- - - - - - - - - - - - - - - - - -

The American Mining Co. was first listed on the N. Y. Stock exchange on Jan. 21.

21. There are other standard editing symbols, but those presented so far in this chapter are sufficient for most editorial purposes in industry. Only one more symbol deserves attention. If you make a change or correction and then change your mind, how do you indicate this? The expression "stet" means "let it stand"; that is, ignore the change.

The subassembly has three relays.

In this example, the editor first hyphenated "subassembly" and then decided (correctly) that the word should be written solid. He canceled the change by writing "stet" near the correction.
Write this edited sentence as the typist should type it.

The Chimpanzee can be a most mischievous pet.

- - - - - - - - - - - - - - -

The chimpanzee can be a mischievous pet.

22. On the next page is a partially complete chart of editing symbols. Complete the chart.

Symbol	Meaning
/	
≡	
⌗	
◡	
	Insert
	Delete
	Transpose
	Move text
	Paragraph
	No paragraph
	Hyphen
	Period
	Spell out
	Ignore change

Symbol	Meaning
/	Lower case
≡	Upper case
#	Space
◡	Close up
∧	Insert
ℐ	Delete
∼	Transpose
⟳	Move text
¶	Paragraph
no ¶	No paragraph
=	Hyphen
⊙	Period
ℓ	Spell out
stet	Ignore change

PREPARING THE FINAL COPY

After you, the editor, have marked the writer's draft, using the standard
editing symbols, the final copy is typed. This final copy is the camera-
ready text from which the plates are made for printing the document;
thus, it is usually called <u>repro</u> (reproducible) copy. The final pages are
also called <u>masters</u>.

Naturally the repro copy will have errors, unless your typist has
superhuman skills. In addition, you might have small changes to make
on the final copy.

You have to use a special non-reproducible pencil for final editing.
The camera does not "see" light blue, so the standard pencil for mark-
ing on masters is the sky blue pencil. If you use any other color (or if
you mark too heavily with the sky blue), the marks will show on the
printed page.

The typist normally makes corrections directly on the final copy
without retyping, unless the changes are extensive. White opaquing
<u>fluid</u>, which dries quickly and provides a surface that can be typed on,

is often used for corrections.   Sometimes adhesive-backed paper is used for pasting in corrections.

Since the editor's final corrections will be very light, a good precaution is to signal the typist by placing a large "X" in either margin opposite the line in which there is a correction.   Some editors also put paper clips on pages that have corrections marked in.

23. Corrections to final copy are normally made with a _____ pencil.

_ _ _ _ _ _ _ _ _ _ _ _ _ _

sky blue

24. What can you do to make sure the typist does not overlook final

corrections? _____

_ _ _ _ _ _ _ _ _ _ _ _ _ _

Indicate the locations of corrections by placing "X's" in the margin. (You can also help by putting paper clips on the pages to be corrected.)

One final note of caution: If you want a technical expert to review the final copy, do not give him the masters; make a xerox copy. Your typist will appreciate this precaution, because if a technical reviewer gets his hands on the repro copy, he may mark it up with something besides sky blue. Or he might spill coffee on it, decorate it with mustard from a ham sandwich, or burn it with a cigarette!

THE EDITOR VERSUS THE WRITER

It can be very difficult to edit another writer's work. Difficult, that is, to edit it while resisting the impulse to rewrite. All editing, if the term is to mean anything more than correcting typographical errors, is to some extent rewriting. A clause must be moved to a better location in the sentence, a cumbersome phrase must be simplified, or a sentence must be restructured to improve clarity. All these things are part of the editorial function, and while a writer might take exception to specific details of the editing, he is not likely to feel that the editor has stepped across the line to invade his own domain.

Equally proficient writers will differ in style, stress, and other nuances of expression. The editor must be constantly on guard not to impose his own style on another writer's work.

25. Here is a sentence from a manuscript that has been submitted for editing.

> Motors from Consolidated Electric Company are superior to Diversified Electronics, Inc., due to better quality control procedures in the case of Consolidated.

Assume that each of the edited versions below is the work of a different editor. Which version is the better example of true editing, as opposed to rewriting?

(a)   Consolidated Electric Company has better quality control procedures than Diversified Electronics, Inc.; therefore, its motors are superior.

(b)   Motors from Consolidated Electric Company are superior to those from Diversified Electronics, Inc. because of better quality control procedures at Consolidated.

— — — — — — — — — — — — — — —

b

Note: You are not expected to decide which version is better writing. Version (b) has necessary changes in wording, but its structure is quite similar to that of the original writing. Of course, the editor is permitted to radically alter the structure if this is necessary. However, version (a) unnecessarily changes the emphasis from "superior motors" to "better quality control."

26. Here is another example of a sentence to be edited.

> The supervisor posted a memorandum which served to remind the crew that everyone had to look after their own tools.

Which of these edited versions is more consistent with the principle of restraint in editing?

(a)   The supervisor posted a memorandum to remind the crew that everyone had to look after his own tools.

(b)   The supervisor of the crew posted a memorandum to remind everyone to look after his own tools.

— — — — — — — — — — — — — —

a

SELF-TEST

These questions will test your understanding of Chapter 8. Answers are given on the following page.

1. Write this sentence as it should appear after the indicated corrections have been made.

   Many americans who never read E. E. Cummings are nevertheless familiar with his name, which noone can deny is unusual.

2. Use standard editing symbols to correct this passage.

   Radio broadcast freqencies are kept with in tolerance through the use of special crystalls. The crystals in an oven are kept because temperture the out put frequency affects.

3. In editing this passage, assume that the first sentence is the end of a paragraph, and "After" starts a new paragraph.

   Leave the bearings in the slovent for at least 20 min. After they have been cleaned, lubri cated, and installed in the sub-assembly, follow the lastest test Procedure, which is dated Aug. 18

4. To cancel an indicated change, write the word _____ near the change.

5. Edit the following passage.

   After the first succesful launching of an American Satellite, some one jokingly remarked "Sputnik was first, but ours smaller." The remark was whimsical however it did emphasize the great advances the Americans have made in sub-miniaturization. The accomplishment Russian in launching the very heavy sputnik was remarkable, but packking hundreds of into a small package components is no mean feat.

6.   In editing final copy, use a _____ pencil.

Answers to Self-Test

If your answers to the test questions do not agree with the ones given
below, review the frames indicated in parentheses after each answer
before you go on to the next chapter.

1.   Many Americans who never read e. e. cummings are nevertheless
     familiar with his name, which no one can deny is unusual.
     (frames 1—11)

2.   Radio broadcast frequencies are kept within tolerance through the
     use of special crystals. The crystals in an oven are kept because
     temperature the output frequency affects. (frames 11, 12, 15, and 16)

3.   Leave the bearings in the solvent for at least 20 min. After they
     have been cleaned, lubricated, and installed in the subassembly,
     follow the latest test procedure, which is dated Aug. 18
     (frames 1, 12, 15, 17, 18, 19, and 20)

4.   stet (frame 21)

5.   After the first successful launching of an American satellite,
     some one jokingly remarked, "Sputnik was first, but ours is smaller."
     The remark was whimsical; however, it did emphasize the great
     advances the Americans have made in subminiaturization. The
     accomplishment Russian in launching the very heavy sputnik was re-
     markable, but packing hundreds of into a small package components
     is no mean feat. (frames 1, 6, 11, 12, 15, 16, and 19)
         Note: If you aren't sure whether a word such as "subminiature"
     should be hyphenated or written solid, the safest course is to check
     a dictionary or the style guide for your company or profession.

6.   sky blue (frame 23)

CHAPTER NINE
Writing Functional Sentences

The heart of good technical writing is good <u>sentences</u>. This chapter will help you to:

- eliminate unnecessary words and phrases;
- avoid incorrect constructions;
- write modifiers that are clear and correct;
- position modifiers correctly;
- emphasize the main thought;
- choose between active and passive voice;
- use parallel constructions.

ELIMINATING USELESS WORDS

Even in ordinary conversation, people appreciate a speaker who can get to the point with an economy of language. When a speaker uses 20 words when 10 would do, the listener automatically edits out the deadwood and usually replies in the same wordy fashion. In writing, however, unnecessary words interfere with clarity, reduce impact, and lull the reader into a glassy-eyed stupor.

1. Examine the following sentence and try to pick out every word that conveys no useful information.

   The attached memorandum is provided for the purpose of information only.

Here is the same sentence with unnecessary words crossed out.

The attached memorandum is ~~provided~~ for ~~the purpose of~~ information only.

Seven words carry the same information as the original 11.

The attached memorandum is for information only. (You might simplify this sentence further by writing, "This memorandum . . .")

Now cross out the useless words in this sentence.

Production was started up three days early in order to meet the new deadline.

– – – – – – – – – – – – – – –

Production was started three days early to meet the new deadline.

2.   The sentence in frame 1 probably didn't look so bad, even before revision, because we are used to phrases like "start up" for "start" and "in order to" for "to." You have to be alert to avoid the excess baggage in even the commonest sentences.
      Try revising this sentence. Write your new sentence in the space provided. (You might practice using the editing symbols you learned earlier as you revise the sentence.)

Connect up the battery cables in order to make use of auxiliary power.

– – – – – – – – – – – – – – –

Connect the battery cables to use auxiliary power.

3.   You often have to change the form of a word to revise a wordy sentence.

The chemist made an analysis of the contaminated solution.

You can improve the sentence by substituting a different verb.

The chemist analyzed the contaminated solution.

Improve this sentence by using the verb forms of "recommendation" and "promotion." Write your new sentence in the space.

The supervisor made the recommendation that the technician be given a promotion.

The supervisor recommended that the technician be promoted.

4. Revise this sentence.

The driver reported bad weather conditions along his route to provide an explanation of his late arrival.

The driver reported bad weather along his route to explain his late arrival.

EXPRESSING MEANINGS CLEARLY

If you use too many words to express your thought, you will waste your reader's time, and you will probably bore and irritate him as well. Using too few words can also cause serious problems, of another sort. Leaving out words, more likely from carelessness than from a desire to be straightforward, can confuse the reader. When the sentence construction is incomplete, the reader might get the meaning through his knowledge of the subject or from the context, but either way he will be slowed down. And he might actually misunderstand what you are trying to say.

5. A word is missing from this sentence.

Weber knows more about nuclear physics than anyone in his section.

Weber is in his section, and he can't know more than he himself knows! The correct wording is "anyone else," not "anyone."

What is missing from this sentence?

Ballard works longer hours than anyone in his department.

_____

– – – – – – – – – – – – – – – –

". . . than anyone <u>else</u> in his department." (You might have said
". . . than the <u>others</u> in his department," but the emphasis would
be slightly less.)

6.   Examine this sentence.

Malley spends more time with the roses than his wife.

You can't really say just what is meant. Perhaps Malley neglects
his wife in favor of the roses; maybe Mrs. Malley doesn't like to
tend the roses. These revisions of the sentence made the meaning
clear.

Malley spends more time with the roses than <u>with</u> his wife.

Malley spends more time with the roses than his wife <u>does</u>.

The simple insertion of "with" or "does" removes the doubt.
Assume that wives do not give presents to their husbands' girl-
friends and revise this sentence.

The actor gave more presents to his girlfriend than his wife.

_____

– – – – – – – – – – – – – – –

". . . than <u>to</u> his wife."

7.   Sometimes the meaning of a sentence is clear, but the construction
is illogical.

The use of aluminum for the framework is preferable to
steel.

We know that the framework should be made of aluminum, not steel,
but "use" is actually compared with "steel." The sentence should
read:

The use of aluminum for the framework is preferable to
<u>that of</u> steel.

You can avoid such illogical constructions by being sure you are comparing what you mean to compare.

Revise this sentence.

Motors from Consolidated Electric Company are superior to Diversified Electronics, Inc.

_____

– – – – – – – – – – – – – – – –

". . . <u>those</u> <u>from</u> Diversified Electronics, Inc."

8. Improve this sentence.

The use of cotton in the lining is inferior to nylon.

_____

– – – – – – – – – – – – – – – –

". . . <u>that</u> <u>of</u> nylon." (You could have said, ". . . to the use of nylon," but this involves unnecessary repetition.)

9. Improve this sentence.

He argued that coffee from Kenya is richer than Guatemala.

_____

– – – – – – – – – – – – – – – –

". . . <u>that</u> <u>from</u> Guatemala."

AVOIDING MISTAKES WITH MODIFIERS

The careless placement of modifying phrases can lead to sentence construction that is sometimes merely humorous, sometimes confusing. The error is compounded when the writer knows what he means to say but neglects to structure the sentence so the reader will also know.

10. This sentence illustrates a common error in the use of modifiers.

Distracted by a billboard, Smith's car crashed into a telephone pole.

Cars can't be distracted; they can't even read. The modifying phrase was meant to modify Smith, but it actually refers to Smith's car.

A simple change of wording corrects the sentence.

Distracted by a billboard, Smith crashed his car into a telephone pole.

Write this sentence so that the meaning is clear.

Driving to the kennel, John's dog jumped out of the car.

– – – – – – – – – – – – – – –

As John was driving to the kennel, his dog jumped out of the car. (You might have used some other wording. The important thing is to make sure "driving" refers to John, rather than to his dog.)

11. The sentence below is incorrect because a burglar can't practice his trade while he is asleep. Revise it.

While sleeping in the bedroom, the burglar made off with Mary's color television set.

– – – – – – – – – – – – – – –

You might have written: While Mary was sleeping in the bedroom, the burglar made off with her color television set. Another possibility is: The burglar made off with Mary's color television set while she was sleeping in the bedroom.

12. "Based on" is an often-used phrase in industry, and it frequently leads to an error that is fairly hard to identify.

Based on extensive market research, the sales manager decided to go ahead with the advertising campaign.

"Based on" actually refers to the sales manager, although the logical reference should be to his decision. The sentence has to be rewritten.

The sales manager's decision to go ahead with the advertising campaign was based on extensive market research.

Of course, there are other ways to say the same thing, but the suggested revision conveys the intended thought.

Try revising this sentence.

Based on an accelerated delivery schedule, the supervisor authorized overtime work for two weeks.

– – – – – – – – – – – – – – –

"Based on" should not modify "supervisor." Here are two possible
revisions.

Faced with an accelerated delivery schedule, the supervisor authorized overtime work for two weeks.

The supervisor authorized overtime work for two weeks to meet an
accelerated delivery schedule.

13. In longer sentences, the modifier is sometimes placed in the middle,
    creating confusion about what is being modified. In this sentence,
    the reader can reason out the function of the plug, but the construc-
    tion is awkward.

    After the pipe is disconnected, using a quarter-inch plug,
    seal the tank.

The plug isn't really used to disconnect the pipe, so we must rewrite
the sentence to make its real function clear.   One possibility is:

    After the pipe is disconnected, use a quarter-inch plug to
    seal the tank.

Here is a different approach.

    Use a quarter-inch plug to seal the tank after the pipe is
    disconnected.

You might prefer still another wording.

    After the pipe is disconnected, seal the tank with a
    quarter-inch plug.

    Try revising the sentence on the next page, bearing in mind that
a solvent is used to clean components, not to inspect them.

After you have inspected the components, using Type A solvent, carefully clean them.

— — — — — — — — — — — — — — —

After you have inspected the components, carefully clean them with Type A solvent.

14. In the next problem sentence, the technician thought the <u>module</u> was operating properly, but there is no way the reader can know for sure. Rewrite the sentence to make this point clear.

After replacing a module, thinking it was operating properly, the technician applied power to the console.

— — — — — — — — — — — — — — —

A suggested revision: After replacing a module, which he thought was operating properly, the technician applied power to the console.

15. Now assume the technician thought the <u>console</u> was operating properly, and make that idea clear in your revision. Here is the original sentence again.

After replacing a module, thinking it was operating properly, the technician applied power to the console.

— — — — — — — — — — — — — — —

After replacing a module, the technician applied power to the console, which he thought was operating properly.

16. Trailing modifiers result when the writer puts down his thoughts without much regard for their proper order and then does not revise.

Wilcox introduced the plan during the week that revolutionized the company's approach to marketing.

The plan was revolutionary, not the week. A little rearrangement makes this clear.

During the week, Wilcox introduced the plan that revolutionized the company's approach to marketing.

Revise this sentence to make it say what it means.

He discovered the trouble after careful investigation that caused the generator to malfunction.

– – – – – – – – – – – – – – – –

You might have written: After careful investigation, he discovered the trouble that caused the generator to malfunction. Give yourself extra points if you simplified the sentence further: After careful investigation, he discovered the cause of the generator malfunction.

17. Assume that running a test program will not make a computer work properly, and revise this sentence.

He concluded that the computer worked properly after running a test program.

– – – – – – – – – – – – – – – –

After running a test program, he concluded that the computer worked properly.

So far we have been concerned with the construction of modifying phrases and clauses to be sure each modifier was correct and clear. English is a positional language, and the meaning of a sentence is changed as the modifier (even if it is only one word) is shifted to different positions in the sentence. A very common modifier is the word "only." Notice in the examples below how the thought can change as "only" is moved to different positions.

Only the designer programmed the new computer. (No one but the designer programmed the new computer.)

The only designer programmed the new computer. (There was only one designer.)

The designer only programmed the new computer. (The designer's act was limited to programming.)

The designer programmed only the new computer. (Someone else programmed the other computers.)

The designer programmed the only new computer. (There was only one new computer.)

As you can see, the modifier should be placed as close as possible to the word it modifies, but even then, it can mislead by seeming to modify the wrong word. In speech, inflection as well as position can help to make the meaning clear. Notice the difference when you emphasize aloud the underscored words in the sentences below.

The designer <u>only</u> programmed the new computer.

The designer only <u>programmed</u> the new computer.

In those spoken sentences, the word order is the same, but the emphasis changes the meaning. In the written version, unless some device such as italics or underscoring is used, the modifier is generally understood to modify the word that follows it.

18. In this sentence, Smith's dealings with the supervisor were limited to argument.

    Smith only argued with the supervisor.

    Rewrite it to express the thought that Smith argued with the supervisor but with no one else.

    _ _ _ _ _ _ _ _ _ _ _ _ _ _ _

    Smith argued only with the supervisor.

19. Now change the sentence in frame 18 to suggest that Smith argued with the supervisor, but no one else did.

    _ _ _ _ _ _ _ _ _ _ _ _ _ _ _

    Only Smith argued with the supervisor.

20. When the modifier is a phrase rather than a single word, the danger of misplacing it is increased. Examine this sentence.

    The relay is located outside the power supply in the control console.

You could get a headache trying to figure out what that sentence really means. Here are the possibilities.

a. The power supply is in the control console, and the relay is located just outside the power supply.

b. The relay is not located in the power supply (which is outside the control console) but is actually inside the control console.

If you wish to express possibility (a), rewrite the sentence something like this.

The relay is located outside the power supply, which is in the control console.

Try rewriting the sentence to suggest that the relay is not housed in the power supply but is in the control console.

- - - - - - - - - - - - - - - - -

The relay is located in the control console rather than in the power supply.
Note: Your version may be substantially different. You really have to know more about the subject. If the relay is associated with the power supply in the mind of the reader, something like this might be better: The relay, although part of the power supply, is actually located in the control console.

21. In the next problem sentence, the capacitors are in the pulse-forming network, but they are not tested there. Rewrite the sentence.

All the capacitors should be tested in the pulse-forming network.

- - - - - - - - - - - - - - - -

All the capacitors in the pulse-forming network should be tested.

22. Revise this sentence.

The laboratory chief told the technicians to calibrate their test instruments at the weekly meeting.

- - - - - - - - - - - - - - - - -

At the weekly meeting, the laboratory chief told the technicians to calibrate their test instruments.

Note: Some other phrasing is all right, as long as the technicians don't calibrate their instruments at the meeting.

STRESSING THE MAIN THOUGHT

Good writing is more than a succession of simple statements. Not all information is equally interesting or valuable to the reader, so main ideas (usually independent clauses) are supported by explanations that tell <u>where</u>, <u>why</u>, <u>when</u>, or <u>how</u> or give some other description.

Here are two simple sentences.

The framework is titanium.

The framework is expensive.

Both thoughts are expressed in each of the following sentences, but the first stresses cost, while the second stresses material.

The titanium framework is expensive.

The expensive framework is titanium.

The main thought usually depends on the point of view. To combine the two statements below, you have to know which is of more interest to the reader.

John missed a week's work.

John had the flu.

John's supervisor might be concerned about his illness, but the problem of a reduced work force is of more pressing importance.

John missed a week's work because he had the flu.

John's wife, though distressed by the thought of a smaller paycheck, is more interested in his health.

John had the flu, which caused him to miss a week's work.

23. From the company's point of view, which sentence more effectively expresses the main thought?

    (a) The construction crew missed its deadline, causing a penalty of $10,000.

    (b) The company had to pay a penalty of $10,000, since the construction crew missed its deadline.

    ‾‾‾‾‾‾‾‾‾‾

    _ _ _ _ _ _ _ _ _ _ _ _ _ _ _

    b. Most companies would probably focus on the loss of the $10,000.

24. Which of these statements is more interesting to a customer?

    (a) Delivery of your turbine will be delayed because our machinists are on strike.

    (b) Our machinists are on strike, so delivery of your turbine will be delayed.

    ‾‾‾‾‾‾‾‾‾‾

    _ _ _ _ _ _ _ _ _ _ _ _ _ _ _

    a. The customer wants his turbine; labor troubles are of secondary importance to him.

25. Assume that bankruptcy is more important than the reasons for it, and revise this sentence.

    The bank did not approve the loan, so the company went bankrupt.

    _ _ _ _ _ _ _ _ _ _ _ _ _ _ _

    Something like: The company went bankrupt because the bank did not approve the loan.

26. Revise the following sentence.

    Figure 2 shows that the control circuit has a secondary power supply.

    _ _ _ _ _ _ _ _ _ _ _ _ _ _

You may have written the sentence in one of many ways.

The control circuit has a secondary power supply, as shown in Figure 2.

The control circuit, shown in Figure 2, has a secondary power supply.

The control circuit (Figure 2) has a secondary power supply.

27. Results are usually more important than the effort that produces them. With this thought in mind, revise this sentence.

The research team ran tests for three weeks, finally isolating the active enzyme.

_ _ _ _ _ _ _ _ _ _ _ _ _ _ _ _

Some suggestions:

The research team, after three weeks of testing, finally isolated the active enzyme.

The research team finally isolated the active enzyme after three weeks of testing.

28. Revise this sentence, which as written stresses the less important thought.

The innocent man fought a long legal battle that ended with his freedom.

_ _ _ _ _ _ _ _ _ _ _ _ _ _ _

Something like: The innocent man won his freedom after a long legal battle.

ACTIVE AND PASSIVE VOICE

Reports, memorandums, and other writings in industry are filled with sentences that are dull, boring, and vague. One of the reasons for this is the abuse of the passive voice in sentence structure. The active voice is direct, while the passive tends to be evasive; the active is vital, while the passive is often lifeless.

There are, of course, situations in which the passive voice is preferable.

I was arrested for running a red light.

Each visitor was given a meal ticket as soon as he arrived.

In the first example, it is clear to almost any reader who did the arresting. The fact of my being arrested is more important than the identity of the arrester, who is assumed to be a police officer. In the second example, it is important to know that each visitor was provided with a meal ticket; less important is the agency from which the visitors received meal tickets.

Far too frequently, however, the passive voice is used when the active voice would be better. Consider the sentences below.

Passive: Help is needed.

Active: I need help.

Note that "I need help" is not a translation of "Help is needed." The translation might be "You need help," or it could be "We need help." That is the point. The passive voice conceals the doer, or true subject of the thought.

Certainly the active voice conveys the greater sense of urgency. It is also more personal (note the pronoun "I" in the example), and many writers automatically use the passive voice because it is impersonal. But the passion for being impersonal is no longer in vogue. Even maintenance manuals, although impersonal in content, are often personal in approach. The imperative ("you" is understood, although not expressed) is usually more effective in instructions.

Passive: The housing is removed.

Active: Remove the housing.

29. Which sentence below is in the active voice?

(a) A good response is expected.

(b) I expect a good response.

– – – – – – – – – – – – – – –

b

30. Which sentence is in the passive voice?

(a) According to the Bible, Jonah was not swallowed by a whale but by a big fish.

(b) The Book of Genesis does not refer to Eve's eating an apple.

_____

– – – – – – – – – – – – – –

a. A sentence in the passive voice can reveal the doer, as this one does, but the key is the word "by" or some similar word.

31. Rewrite this sentence in the active voice.

Three control relays are incorporated in the circuit.

– – – – – – – – – – – – – –

The circuit incorporates three control relays.
    Note: You could further improve the sentence by saying: The circuit has three control relays.

32. Rewrite this sentence in the active voice.

The company was praised in the <u>Time</u> article.

– – – – – – – – – – – – –

The <u>Time</u> article praised the company.
    Note: Technically, it was the author of the article who praised the company, not the article itself, but you needn't bore the reader with unnecessary technicalities.

The passive voice is sometimes necessary, but writers often use it because it seems more tactful. Sometimes, however, being tactful results in a sentence which is not only confusing, but dull and unnatural.

<u>It</u> <u>is</u> <u>recommended</u> that the special tools <u>be</u> <u>purchased.</u>

The passive voice forces a more wordy construction, and it also gives less direct information. Who recommends? Who will purchase the tools? The reader might know from the context, but why not say so? The active voice requires the doer to be named.

I recommend that we purchase the special tools.

The passive voice also seems to discourage simple words. "Be purchased" fits the style of the sentence better than "be bought." But in the active voice, the simpler word is natural.

I recommend that we buy the special tools.

"Let's buy the special tools" is even more forceful, but that's a little too informal for most industrial writing.

A great many sentences in industrial writing start with "It is" or "It was," thus concealing the doer. If the actor is named, a phrase is required instead of a single word.

Passive: It was recommended by the supervisor that Miller be promoted.

Active:　The supervisor recommended Miller's promotion.

33. Rewrite this sentence in the active voice.

It is suggested by all available evidence that reliability will be increased by the use of an auxiliary power supply.

— — — — — — — — — — — — — — —

All available evidence suggests that an auxiliary power supply will increase reliability.

34. It would be a mistake to think the passive voice is never preferable. Technical writing often deals with material in which the agent is not important.

The testing was completed two days early.

Peak voltage is reached in 20 microseconds.

The circuit is completed when relay K-23 closes.

In the following sentence, it is important to know that rats were used in testing the virus, but who ran the tests is superfluous. Rewrite the sentence.

Researchers used five white rats in testing the mutated virus.

— — — — — — — — — — — — — — —

Some possibilities:

Five white rats were used in testing the mutated virus.

The mutated virus was injected into five white rats.

    Note: You weren't told that the virus was injected. The second sentence was added to show you how additional useful detail can be easily added.

35. Rewrite this sentence.

A temperature of 200 F causes the alarm to sound.

_ _ _ _ _ _ _ _ _ _ _ _ _ _ _

One suggestion: The alarm sounds at 200 F.
    Note: Since "200 F" indicates temperature, it is not necessary to use the word "temperature" in the sentence.

PARALLEL CONSTRUCTIONS

Good writing should show relationships. Awkward or careless sentence structure, although grammatically correct, can easily obscure rather than stress relationships. The best way to clearly bring out relationships is to use parallelism of construction. That is, say similar things in similar ways.

    In simple sentences, relationships are clear regardless of parallelism, but parallel constructions are neater.

Not parallel: The robber was shifty-eyed and had a snub nose.

Parallel: The robber was shifty-eyed and snub-nosed.

Parallel: The robber had shifty eyes and a snub nose.

36. Revise this sentence to make the construction parallel.

She was golden-haired and had dancing blue eyes.

_ _ _ _ _ _ _ _ _ _ _ _ _ _ _

She had golden hair and dancing blue eyes.

37. Parallel construction often clarifies more complex sentences. For example, one clause is often written in the active voice and another in the passive. The sentence can be made parallel by writing each clause in the same voice.

> Not parallel: A circuit breaker protects the power supply, while the amplifier circuits are protected by fuses.

> Parallel: A circuit breaker protects the power supply, while fuses protect the amplifier circuits.

> Parallel: The power supply is protected by a circuit breaker, while the amplifier circuits are protected by fuses.

Make the clauses in this sentence parallel, first by using only the active voice, then by using only the passive voice.

A yellow light indicates the STANDBY condition, and the OPERATE condition is indicated by a green light.

Active:

Passive:

— — — — — — — — — — — — — — —

Active: A yellow light indicates the STANDBY condition, and a green light indicates the OPERATE condition.

Passive: The STANDBY condition is indicated by a yellow light, and the OPERATE condition is indicated by a green light.

Note: Right now we are concerned only with parallelism, but you could simplify that sentence in a number of ways. One is by elision: A yellow light indicates STANDBY; a green light, OPERATE.

38. You don't have to get involved in grammatical terminology to analyze a sentence for parallelism. Can you figure out why this sentence is not parallel?

> The design of the motor is described in Section 1 and how it operates, in Section 2.

The comparison of "design" with "how it operates" is not parallel.

Substitute "operation" for "how it operates."

> The design of the motor is described in Section 1; its operation, in Section 2.

Revise this sentence.

The brochure describes the history of the company as well as how it is organized at present.

— — — — — — — — — — — — — — —

The brochure describes the history of the company as well as its present organization.

39. Revise this sentence.

Good dental health requires brushing after every meal, be careful of sweets, and you should get regular checkups.

— — — — — — — — — — — — — —

Two suggestions:

Good dental health requires brushing after every meal, being careful of sweets, and getting regular checkups.

For good dental health, you should brush after every meal, be careful of sweets, and get regular checkups.

SELF-TEST

These questions will test your understanding of Chapter 9. Answers are given on the following page.

Each of the following sentences contains one or more of the faults discussed in this chapter. Improve each sentence in any manner you feel is appropriate and write your revised sentence in the space provided below each faulty sentence. The revisions provided in the answers are only suggestions. In some cases, your own wording probably will be different; it may even be better.

1. Jones married on December 31 in order to gain an extra exemption and get a reduction in his income tax.

2. Nutritionists are more aware than anyone that eating eggs for breakfast is preferable to cereal.

3. Walking against the light, the cab driver missed the woman narrowly.

4. Based on a careless estimate of costs, the company lost money on the bid.

5. The mechanic only lubricated the bearings. (Hint: He didn't lubricate anything else.)

6. He located the defective cam in the drive assembly that caused the trouble.

7. A spark-gap switch failed to close, causing the beam-forming assembly to misfire.

8. Half the crew missed work due to the flu epidemic, and the fabrication department could not finish the job on time.

9. It was voted by the recreation committee that the company picnic be canceled.

10. Symptoms of shock include shallow, irregular breathing, and the skin is moist and cool.

Answers to Self-Test

If your answers to the test questions do not agree with the ones given below, you may wish to review the chapter. Specific frame references are not given for review because questions are drawn from many parts of the chapter.

1. Jones married on December 31 to gain an extra exemption and reduce his income tax.

2. Nutritionists are more aware than anyone else that eating eggs for breakfast is preferable to eating cereal.

3. The cab driver narrowly missed the woman, who was walking against the light.

4. The company lost money on the bid, which was based on a careless estimate of costs.

5. The mechanic lubricated only the bearings. (The original sentence implies that something else needed to be done to the bearings.)

6. He located the defective cam, which caused the trouble, in the drive assembly. (The cam, not the drive assembly, caused the trouble.)

7. The beam-forming assembly misfired because a spark-gap switch failed to close. (The emphasis should be on the misfiring of the beam-forming assembly.)

8. The fabrication department could not finish the job on time, since half the crew missed work because of the flu epidemic. (The phrase "due to" in the original sentence is incorrect. "Since" was substituted for "because" to avoid repetition of that word.)

9. The recreation committee voted to cancel the company picnic.

10. Symptoms of shock include shallow, irregular breathing and moist, cool skin.

CHAPTER TEN
Words and Phrases

There was a fad, some years ago, of clothing well-known sayings in high-flown language, just for the fun of it. "Too many cooks spoil the broth," for example, was translated into something like "A superfluity of culinary artists renders worthless the consomme."

Many of the participants seem to have slipped into business and industry without realizing it was all a joke. Actual passages in technical and professional writing might not be quite as bad as the following passage, but some of them come close.

> In the event that you are desirous of registering your objection to the finalized version of the contract at this point in time, it is necessary that you enter into a conference with the people who represent us prior to the time when negotiations have progressed to a conclusion.

This gobbledygook really means:

> If you want to object to the final contract now, you must confer with our representatives before negotiations have ended.

Almost everyone in industry has been brainwashed by this kind of language to the point where it sometimes cannot be recognized as ludicrous. "Officialese" is a way of life, and it is up to the writer to avoid such cumbersome language.

Much of the English language is based on Latin, and many words come from Greek. Those Latin- and Greek-based words are in the language because they are useful and have specific meanings. It is not the use but the abuse of them that is objectionable. Even many highly educated people are not really comfortable with Latin. It is not surprising that they often make mistakes in using words like "comprise" and "infer." Check into the etymology of the common, everyday words in the language, and you will find that most of them are Anglo-Saxon or

Germanic—the most important ancestors of common English. The words are clear and they have great vitality. If they are adequate to express your thoughts, don't hesitate to use them. Use "before" instead of "prior to," "main" instead of "principal," and so forth.

Officialese, misuse of words, and vague phrasing are three major obstacles to clear communication; there are others. They will be analyzed in an attempt to help you keep them out of your writing.

When you have finished this chapter, you will be able to:

- recognize, and therefore avoid, the cumbersome phraseology that is the heart of officialese;

- avoid the misuse of many words commonly found in technical writing;

- choose phrasing that is direct and forceful rather than awkward, vague, and weak;

- recognize and avoid redundancies;

- eliminate words and phrases that convey no information.

AVOIDING CUMBERSOME PHRASES

Technical and professional people are exposed on every side to wordy phrases that obstruct meaning. Even when the writer tries to avoid it, wordiness creeps in. There are two steps to the solution: Try to use the simple word or two, rather than the cumbersome word or phrase, when you write your first draft; then go back and edit ruthlessly.

It is impossible to list all cumbersome phrases, but by analyzing some of the frequently occurring ones, you can develop an attitude of awareness. That is what is really needed. You can also learn the simple equivalents for some of the wordy phrases you encounter here.

A prime example of wordiness is "in the event that." It almost always means "if" and nothing else. Why would anybody want to improve on a word like "if"? Perhaps it stems from a closely related phrase for which there is slightly more justification: "In the unlikely event that . . ."

The next few frames are designed to help you find simple substitutes for cumbersome phrases.

1. Select appropriate words from the list below and substitute them for
    underlined phrases in the following sentence. Write your simplified
    sentence in the space provided.
        requires
        if
        tend

    In the event that the bearings exhibit a tendency to stick, proper
    maintenance involves the necessity of cleaning with a standard
    solvent.

    – – – – – – – – – – – – – – –

    If the bearings tend to stick, proper maintenance requires cleaning
    with a standard solvent.

2. The sentence in frame 1 is still more wordy than it needs to be.
    Forget the philosophy about proper maintenance and tell the reader
    what to do. (Hint: Use the phrase "clean them" in the sentence
    you write.)

    – – – – – – – – – – – – – – –

    If the bearings tend to stick, clean them with a standard solvent.

3. Select appropriate words from the list below and substitute them for
    underlined phrases in the following sentence.
        with
        near
        using

    The mobile loading dock was brought into close proximity to the
    warehouse doors by the utilization of a jacking arrangement in
    conjunction with steel supports.

    – – – – – – – – – – – – – – –

    The mobile loading dock was brought near the warehouse doors by
    using a jacking arrangement with steel supports.

4. Select appropriate words or phrases from the list below and substitute them for underlined phrases in the following sentence.

    because
    by air
    to meet

The parts were shipped <u>by means of air transportation for the purpose of meeting</u> the delivery date <u>for the simple reason that</u> the railway workers were on strike.

– – – – – – – – – – – – –

The parts were shipped <u>by air to meet</u> the delivery date <u>because</u> the railway workers were on strike.

5. Select appropriate words or phrases from the list below and substitute them for underlined phrases in the following sentence.

    had to   while
    many   talk to
    about

I <u>found it necessary to confer with</u> the shop steward <u>with reference to</u> the <u>large number of</u> grievances that were reported <u>during the time that</u> I was away from the plant.

– – – – – – – – – – – – –

I <u>had to talk to</u> the shop steward <u>about</u> the <u>many</u> grievances that were reported <u>while</u> I was away from the plant.

6. Reword the following sentence, simplifying it while retaining the original meaning.

<u>Due to the fact that</u> the beryllium alloy is <u>in short supply, it is within the realm of possibility that</u> we may <u>be faced with the necessity of engaging in a search</u> for a satisfactory substitute.

– – – – – – – – – – – – –

<u>Because</u> the beryllium alloy is <u>scarce</u>, we <u>may have to look</u> for a satisfactory substitute.

7. Rewrite the following sentence, simplifying cumbersome phraseology without changing the meaning.

    At this point in time we have in excess of 200 percent spare parts, but we may be faced with the necessity of purchasing an additional number of parts prior to the end of the fiscal year.

    — — — — — — — — — — — — — — — —

    We now have more than 200 percent spare parts, but we may need to purchase more parts before the end of the fiscal year.

MISUSE OF WORDS

8. Industrial and professional writings are filled with examples of the misuse of words. The confusion between "imply" and "infer" is classic. Writers rarely misuse "imply," but "infer" is quite a different story. The following sentence is typical.

    His statement inferred that the fabrication department is behind schedule.

    The correct word is "implied." To imply is to give an impression; to infer is to receive an impression. You might infer something that I did not intend to imply.
    Select the appropriate words in the following sentences.

    (a) Did you mean to _____, in your introduction, that your
                               (imply/infer)
         research was entirely independent?

    (b) I _____ from your comment that you were thinking
            (inferred/implied)
         of taking another job.

    — — — — — — — — — — — — — — —

    (a) imply; (b) inferred

9. Many writers confuse "affect" and "effect." We need not be concerned with the noun form of "affect," because it is rarely used. The verb means to influence. "Effect" has both noun and verb forms; the verb means to bring about, while the noun means a result.

Here are examples of the proper use of "affect" and "effect."

Affect (verb): You should not let personal bias affect your decision.

Effect (verb): After hours of negotiation, they were able to effect a compromise.

Effect (noun): Increased imports are bound to have an effect on the price of domestic goods.

Select the appropriate words in the following sentences.

(a) An unhappy employee can _____ the morale of an
    (affect/effect)
    entire section.

(b) The _____ of hydrogen on chrome plating is well known.
    (affect/effect)

(c) Sales of the new desk calculator should _____ an increase
    (affect/effect)
    of profits of at least 10 percent.

- - - - - - - - - - - - - - -

(a) affect; (b) effect; (c) effect

10. "Less" is often required to do double duty, unless the writer is careful. Consider the two sentences below.

His bonus was less than half what he had expected.

Less than six men applied for the position.

In the first sentence, "less" is correct, because it refers to a general quantity that cannot be counted out. Six men can be counted, however, so the correct word is "fewer," not "less," in the second sentence. Select the correct words in the following sentences.

(a) The typist made _____ mistakes than anyone else in the
    (less/fewer)
    office.

(b) The new contract provided for a little more money but

    _____ holidays.
    (less/fewer)

- - - - - - - - - - - - - - -

(a) fewer; (b) fewer

11. The use of "and/or" is borrowed from legal writing and is rarely, if ever, required in technical writing; the writer should use the single word that applies. To use both is overkill and interferes with the smooth flow of the sentence. Look at this example.

> The job requires an engineering degree and/or 4 years' experience.

If 4 years' experience is an acceptable alternative to the degree, the "and" is unnecessary and misleading. If both the degree and the experience are required, the "or" is incorrect.
Consider this example.

> Use a nonferrous metal such as copper and/or aluminum.

Aside from the grammatical problem often presented by "and/or," the above example clearly calls for "or" alone, since either copper or aluminum is nonferrous.
Look at still another example.

> Vitamin A can be obtained from many fruits and/or vegatables.

In this case, "and" alone is correct, because both fruits and vegetables contain Vitamin A. The "or" is pointless.
The "and/or" is more likely to occur when either or both of two conditions can produce an effect.

> An airplane will stall when the airspeed decreases sufficiently and/or when the angle of attack is sufficiently increased.

But "and/or" is not correct. It seems to be correct, because there are interacting variables: an airplane flying at a given angle of attack will stall when the airspeed drops sufficiently, or it will stall without a change in airspeed if the angle of attack is increased sufficiently. Since either of the two conditions is alone sufficient to cause a stall, the "and" is pointless.
Make this test for yourself: In any sentence containing the term "and/or," try substituting first "and" and then "or." Select the word which leaves the intended sense of the sentence unchanged.
An increase in atmospheric pressure causes an increase in air density; a decrease in temperature also causes an increase in air density. Assuming these two facts, rewrite the sentence on the next page.

An increase in atmospheric pressure and/or a decrease in temperature will cause an increase in air density.

- - - - - - - - - - - - - - - -

An increase in atmospheric pressure <u>or</u> a decrease in temperature will cause an increase in air density.

12. An overworked (and usually incorrect) phrase is "due to." To be correct, "due to" must be immediately preceded by a form of the verb "to be," such as "is" or "were." Otherwise, use "because of." Look at the examples below.

> Wrong: Delivery will be delayed one day, due to the holiday.

> Right: Delivery will be delayed one day because of the holiday.

In this example, "due to" is used correctly.

The delay in delivery was due to the unexpected holiday.

Rewrite this sentence.

Traffic was backed up for miles, due to the overturned trailer on the highway.

- - - - - - - - - - - - - - - -

Traffic was backed up for miles because of the overturned trailer on the highway.

13. What could be simpler than the straightforward word "before"? But technical and professional people consistently favor the phrase "prior to." "Before" is almost always preferable.
Simplify this sentence.

Read the instructions prior to starting the experiment.

- - - - - - - - - - - - - - - -

Read the instructions before starting the experiment.

14. The three words below should be examined and their real meanings understood.

consist   compose   comprise

They are often used interchangeably by writers, although they should not be. In almost no case will misuse of any of these words mislead the reader, because the context makes the meaning clear. If the reader is alert and well-informed, however, his respect for the writer might be diminished. The following sentence illustrates the meanings of these three words.

Air $\begin{cases} \text{consists of} \\ \text{comprises} \\ \text{is composed of} \end{cases}$ oxygen, nitrogen, and trace gases.

You cannot correctly write "is comprised of," yet this is frequently done, perhaps from analogy with "is composed of." "Comprise" means "embrace." The subject of "comprise" is the whole, not the parts.

Rewrite the following sentence using some form of "comprise" in place of the phrase "is composed of."

The clerical staff is composed of typists, file clerks, and a supervisor.

- - - - - - - - - - - - - - - -

The clerical staff comprises typists, file clerks, and a supervisor.

USING STANDARD VERBS

A process that etymologists call "back-formation" has produced many verbs in technical writing that serve no useful purpose, because simpler equivalents already exist. Here are some examples.

Standard Verb	Noun	New Verb
orient	orientation	orientate
administer	administration	administrate
filter	filtration	filtrate

These new verbs, and others, have actually found their way into dictionaries, which reflect usage, but that is no excuse for using them. If you do find such words in your first draft, you can improve your writing by striking them out and using the original verbs.

If we are not alert to this trend of back-formation, we should not be surprised to encounter such words as "presentate, refutate, and revelate" for "present, refute, and reveal."

15. Substitute standard verbs for the back-formations in these sentences.

    (a) A newcomer often has trouble orientating himself in this maze of offices.

    _____

    (b) A professor from New York City College was appointed to administrate the scholarship fund.

    _____

    (c) The solution should be filtrated to remove sediment.

    _____

— — — — — — — — — — — — — — —

(a) orienting in place of orientating
(b) administer in place of administrate
(c) filtered in place of filtrated

16. Two common non-words are "irregardless" and "re-occur." "Irregardless" is used because the writer attaches the negative prefix "ir-" without noticing that there is already a negative suffix, "-less." Correct this sentence.

The Division Manager decided to go ahead with the program irregardless of the added expense.

— — — — — — — — — — — — — — —

. . . regardless of the added expense.

17. "Re-occur" is an awkward back-formation from "occur." It is used because writers and speakers either don't know or forget that there is a better word: recur.

Correct this sentence.

The physicist performed the experiment several times, but he could not detect a re-occurrence of the phenomenon.

- - - - - - - - - - - - - - -

. . . detect a recurrence of the phenomenon.

18. Rewrite this passage.

The line losses were greatly diminished when the transmission line was reorientated 90 degrees clockwise. The new orientation, however, caused a new problem with stray capacitance, which re-occurred during peak loads, irregardless of the position of the cables.

- - - - - - - - - - - - - - -

The line losses were greatly diminished when the transmission line was reoriented 90 degrees clockwise. The new orientation, however, caused a new problem with stray capacitance, which recurred during peak loads, regardless of the position of the cables.

CHOOSING FORCEFUL VERBS

Verbs, not nouns, are the backbone of a language; they give the language meaning and vitality. The problem, in technical writing, stems from the fact that hundreds of verbs have noun forms: purify, purification; install installation; apply, application. These nouns are not only useful but essential when used properly, but they should not be expected to do the work of verbs. Nevertheless, writers try to impose this burden on them, and the result is the use of two verbs which, in combination, have far less force than the single original verb.

Many technical writers are fascinated by, or careless about, these noun forms of verbs. Whatever the reason, such writers constantly use phrases such as "make an installation," "give an indication," and "bring to a conclusion," instead of the simple verbs, "install," "indicate," and "conclude."

Professor H. J. Tichy, author of <u>Effective</u> <u>Writing</u> <u>for</u> <u>Engineers</u>, <u>Managers</u>, <u>Scientists</u>, * has made a thorough analysis of this practice of diluting verbs by using another verb with the noun form of the original verb. (She also notes other combinations that include adjectives or unnecessary words.) Study her list of "dilute verbs," with the suggested improvements, before you try on your own to clean up some examples of technical writing. The list is provided on the next three pages of this book.

---

*A hardcover book, published by John Wiley & Sons, that I highly recommend.

DILUTE VERB	SUGGESTION	EXAMPLE	
achieve purification	Use *purify*.	*Wordy:*	An expert will achieve purification of this water.
		Improved:	An expert will purify this water.
are found to be in agreement	Use *agree*.	*Wordy:*	The values are found to be in agreement.
		Improved:	The values agree.
analyses were made	Use *analyze*.	*Wordy:*	Analyses were made of each sample.
		Improved:	Each sample was analyzed.
is applicable	Use *applies*.		
carry on the work of developing	Use *develop*.		
connection is made	Use *connects*.	*Wordy:*	The connection is made by pipes. . . .
		Improved:	Pipes connect. . . .
carry out, has been carried out	Avoid this phrase when nothing is carried.	*Wordy:*	The installation of the television station has been carried out.
		Improved:	The television station was installed.
carry out experiments	Use *experiment*.		
carry out mixing	Use *mix*.		
carry out purification	Use *purify*.		
is characterized by has the character of	Use *be* or *have* or *resemble* or *look like* when suitable.	*Wordy:*	Her work is characterized by errors.
		Improved:	Her work has many errors.
			Her work is inaccurate.
		Wordy:	This element has the character of several less common elements.
		Improved:	This element resembles several less common ones.

DILUTE VERB	SUGGESTION	EXAMPLE	
bring to a conclusion	Use *conclude, complete, end, finish.*		
is corrective of	Use *corrects.*		
arrive at a decision	Use *decide,* at least sometimes. Occasionally one must decide without the delay suggested by *arrive at.*		
determine detection	Use *detect* or *determine.*	*Wordy:*	The detection of x is determined by the method.
		Improved:	We detect x by the method. The method determines x.
failed to find	Use the negative, at least occasionally.	*Wordy:*	They have failed to find an answer.
		Improved:	They have not found an answer.
is found to be	Use *be.*	*Wordy:*	The recommendation is found to be preferable.
		Improved:	This recommendation is preferable.
give an indication of	Use *indicate.*		
give proof of	Use *prove.*		
give a weakness to	Use *weaken.*	*Wordy:*	This finding gives a weakness to his conclusions.
		Improved:	This finding weakens his conclusions.
is indicative of	Use *indicate.*	*Wordy:*	This is indicative of carelessness.
		Improved:	This indicates carelessness.
institute an improvement in	Use *improve.*	*Wordy:*	His method would institute an improvement in the process.
		Improved:	His method would improve the process.
are known to be, is known to be	Use *are* or *is* except in rare instances.	*Wordy:*	The reaction time is known to be unreliable.
		Improved:	The reaction time is unreliable.
		Exception:	Although the readings of this operator are known to be reliable, he insists upon checking them.

DILUTE VERB	SUGGESTION	EXAMPLE	
make adjustments to	Use *adjust.*		
make an approximation of	Use *approximate.*		
make an examination of	Use *examine.*		
make an exception of	Use *except.*		
make mention of	Use *mention.*		
make out a list	Use *list.*		
make a study of	Use *study.*		
obtain an increase or decrease in temperature	Use *raise* or *lower* temperature.		
are of the opinion that	*Think that* and *believe that* are briefer.	*Wordy:*	We are of the opinion that the process is economical.
		Improved:	We think that the process is economical.
perform an examination of	Use *examine.*		
proceed to separate	Use *separate.*		
present a conclusion	Use *conclude* if that is what you mean.		
present a report	Use *report.*		
present a summary	Use *summarize.*		
put to use in (building, measuring, purifying, etc.)	Use *build, measure, purify; used for building, measuring, purifying.*	*Wordy:*	The old wood was put to use in building the garage.
		Improved:	The old wood was used to build the garage. *or* He built the garage of the old wood.
was seen, was noted	In many sentences these are unnecessary and weak.	*Wordy:*	A large increase in volume was seen.
		Improved:	Volume increased by 2,500 sales.
		Wordy and weak:	The temperature was noted to be 103°F. This suggested that . . . .
		Improved:	The temperature of 103°F suggested that . . . .
succeed in doing, in making, in measuring, in estimating, etc.	Omit *succeed in.* Use *do, make, measure, estimate,* etc.		
is suggestive of	Use *suggests.*		
take cognizance of	Use *note, notice, heed.*		
take into consideration	Use *consider.*		
undertake a study of	Use *study.*		

19. Rewrite the following sentence, using a simpler and more direct construction.

The study provided a clear demonstration of the growth of sales in the Midwest.

— — — — — — — — — — — — — — —

The study clearly demonstrated the growth of sales in the Midwest.

20. Rewrite this sentence.

He made application for a loan to bring about the development of a new apartment complex.

— — — — — — — — — — — — — — —

He applied for a loan to develop a new apartment complex.

21. Rewrite this sentence.

A private detective was hired to carry out an investigation of the new manager's background.

— — — — — — — — — — — — — — —

A private detective was hired to investigate the new manager's background.

22. You can really do a pruning job on this passage.

This medical statement is indicative of the fact that you are engaging in too much work. We are of the opinion that you are in need of a vacation and make the recommendation that you make the arrangements for some time off at the earliest opportunity.

— — — — — — — — — — — — —

Your version is sure to be somewhat different from mine, but here is one possibility:

This medical statement indicates that you are working too hard. We think you need a vacation and recommend that you arrange for some time off at once.

REDUNDANCIES AND MEANINGLESS WORDS

Few people really "edit" their speech, and redundancies—the needless repetition of ideas in other words—are commonplace. You can and should edit your writing, however, to get rid of repetitive words and phrases. All that is really required is a little thought about the <u>meaning</u> of what you write. The list of common redundancies in writing is almost endless, but a few examples should suffice to help you recognize the problem.

<u>Redundancy</u>	<u>Comment</u>
red in color	Can something be red in shape?
basic fundamentals	Aren't fundamentals basic?

Other expressions include redundancies that are not quite so obvious.

plan ahead plan in advance	Plans can be made only for the future.
circulate around	"Around" is included in "circulate."
psychogenic in origin	The suffix "-genic" implies origin.
just exactly like	"Just like" or "exactly like."

23. Rewrite this sentence to remove the redundancy.

He failed to heed the advance warning.

— — — — — — — — — — — — — —

Delete "advance."

24. Rewrite this sentence.

A good hostess must circulate around among her guests.

— — — — — — — — — — — — —

Delete "around."

25. Rewrite this sentence.

The program requires the mutual cooperation of all employees.

— — — — — — — — — — — — —

Delete "mutual." It is implied in "cooperation."

26. Rewrite this sentence.

The nodules were gray in color and weighed in the range of 10 to 20 grams.

— — — — — — — — — — — — —

The nodules were gray and weighed 10 to 20 grams. (The phrase "10 to 20" implies a range.)

27. Rewrite this sentence.

His speech was brief in duration.

— — — — — — — — — — — — —

Delete "in duration." "Brief" implies duration.

In dealing with redundancies, you deleted words and phrases that conveyed no additional information; that is, they were repetitive. Other words and phrases convey no information and merely clutter up the sentence. In the examples on the next page, the useless words are in parentheses.

We must decide (as to) whether to renew his contract.

The compound is not usable (at) above 200 F.

Connect (up) the negative lead to the output terminal.

He forgot to empty (out) the tank.

Mr. Hulet was chosen to head (up) the department.

The two sections should be joined (together) with epoxy.

Take that motor off (of) the table.

There is no way all these unnecessary words can be covered systematically, but the next few frames will at least make you aware of them.

28. Delete any unnecessary words in this sentence.

The design engineer will have to decide as to whether the generator should be connected up today.

— — — — — — — — — — — — — —

Delete "as to," "up."

29. Delete any unnecessary words.

Leave the report on top of my desk and file it away later on.

— — — — — — — — — — — — — —

Leave the report on my desk and file it later.

30. Delete any unnecessary words.

Use butyl rubber gaskets to seal off the tanks before you open up the input valve.

— — — — — — — — — — — — — —

Delete "off," "up."

Such phrases as "there are," "there is," and "in the case of" no doubt have their place in the language, but technical writers should look at them carefully. Such introductory phrases usually weaken the statements they introduce. Look at the example below.

> There are six objectives listed in the preamble to the Constitution. They are: to form a more perfect union . . .

It is much better to get directly to the point.

> The six objectives listed in the preamble to the Constitution are: to form a more perfect union . . .

Here is another example of a wordy (and weak) construction.

> In the case of private polls, it was shown that the candidate had little chance of winning.

Not only is "in the case of" an unnecessary phrase, but it forces the rest of the sentence into the passive voice, which not only weakens the statement but adds more words. If you make "private polls" the subject of your sentence (it is certainly the subject of your thought), your sentence is greatly improved.

> Private polls showed that the candidate had little chance of winning.

31. Rewrite the following sentence to make a more direct statement.

> In the case of interviews with ghetto dwellers, it was indicated that a great many would refuse to move to other neighborhoods.

- - - - - - - - - - - - - - - -

> Interviews with ghetto dwellers indicated that a great many would refuse to move to other neighborhoods.
>   Note: If you simplified further by deleting "a great," you have the right idea, but the sense is somewhat changed.

32. Rewrite the following passage.

> There are three Benelux nations. They are Belgium, Netherlands, and Luxembourg.

- - - - - - - - - - - - - - - -

The three Benelux nations are Belgium, Netherlands, and Luxembourg.

33. Rewrite the following passage.

It might be expected that there could be some disagreement with your plan.

- - - - - - - - - - - - - - -

Something like: Some disagreement with your plan might be expected. Or: You might expect some disagreement with your plan.

Many technical and professional people, no matter how forthright they might be in their speech, seem to evade, qualify, and hedge when they write. Here is an example.

Speech: I think we should delay the project.

Writing: In my opinion, it might possibly be better to consider some delay in initiating the project.

The horrible example is probably exaggerated a little, but not much. Such circumlocution (the word really means "talking around") is probably used by writers to avoid the appearance of being opinionated. The result is that they merely appear timid and uncertain.

34. Rewrite this sentence. (Hint: Use some form of "seem.")

There is some indication that the phenomenon is very unique.

- - - - - - - - - - - - - - -

The phenomenon seems unique.
    Note: Either something is unique, or it is not. "Very unique" is always incorrect. Don't qualify absolutes ("more unique," "very essential"); to do so is illogical, and the statement is weakened.

35. Rewrite this sentence.

It is quite probable that his substandard performance is of a temporary nature.

_ _ _ _ _ _ _ _ _ _ _ _ _ _ _ _

Something like: His substandard performance is probably temporary.

SELF-TEST

These questions will test your understanding of Chapter 10. Answers are given on the following page.

Rewrite the following passages, applying the principles outlined in this chapter. You may delete words and phrases, reword, or otherwise change the construction to give the sentences greater simplicity, clarity, and directness. In each case, the new sentence or passage must retain the sense of the original.

1. In the event that the project involves the necessity of your traveling out of town, you will be afforded an opportunity of drawing an advance against pay.

2. He found it necessary to negotiate with a large number of former colleagues during the time that the merger was being arranged.

3. They had to make a request for reservations a week prior to their visit, due to the two large conventions in the city.

4. Your statement inferred that there was nothing we could do to effect the morale in the plant, but we are here for the purpose of trying anyway.

5. The heads of departments had a meeting for the purpose of making a decision with reference to the work force. They had to make a reduction in overhead expenses and/or employ less workers.

6. The construction crew is comprised of a large number of immigrants who are not yet orientated to working a 40-hour week.

7. The physician made an examination of the patient three days subsequent to the initial visit, but the original symptoms did not re-occur.

8. A wise student must plan ahead for the purpose of taking the college entrance examinations by making a thorough study of the basic fundamentals of mathematics during the time that he is still in high school.

9. The construction chief had to make a decision as to whether the work could be brought to a conclusion in time.

10. There are only two physicists on the list. They are Dr. Burns and Mr. Smith.

11. It is quite probable that we can bring about an improvement in efficiency by means of firing the foreman.

Answers to Self-Test

Some phrasing and choices of words in your sentences will, of course, differ from the versions suggested here. But if you left some wordy phrases unchanged, you may want to review the frames indicated in parentheses following each answer.

1. If the project requires you to travel out of town, you may draw an advance against pay. (frames 1—7)

2. He had to negotiate with many former colleagues while the merger was being arranged. (frames 1—7)

3.　They had to request reservations a week before their visit because of the two large conventions in the city. (frames 12, 19—22)

4.　Your statement implied that we could no nothing to affect the morale in the plant, but we are here to try anyway. (frames 4, 8, and 9)

5.　The heads of departments met to decide about the work force. They either had to reduce overhead expenses or employ fewer workers. (frames 4, 5, 10, and 11)

6.　The construction crew comprises (. . . consists of, . . . is composed of) many immigrants who are not yet oriented to working a 40-hour week. (frames 14 and 15)

7.　The physician examined the patient three days after the first visit, but the original symptoms did not recur. (frames 16, 19—22)

8.　A wise student plans for the college entrance examinations by thoroughly studying the fundamentals of mathematics while he is in high school. (frames 1—7, and 23—30)

9.　The construction chief had to decide whether the work could be concluded in time. (frames 5, 19—22)

10.　The only two physicists on the list are Dr. Burns and Mr. Smith. (frames 31—33)

11.　We can probably improve efficiency by firing the foreman. (frames 1—7, 34, and 35)

PART THREE
Basic Documents

Part Three describes some principal documents that are standard throughout industry. These chapters are not programmed because they are intended for your general information and reference, rather than for teaching you about material.

The principles of technical writing apply to all the documents described, but there are differences in style, format, and basic approach.
In fact, you will note several departures from the guidelines suggested
in this book. In many cases you will be guided by existing specifications
and company guidelines, but if you have the freedom to develop your own
style and format in writing a particular document, Part Three will help.

CHAPTER ELEVEN

Manuals

This chapter will illustrate format for two types of manual: the technical manual and the planning or policy manual.

The typical technical manual provides information necessary to operate and maintain some kind of hardware, from a single piece of equipment to an entire system. The primary users of technical manuals are the operators of the equipment and the technicians who must maintain it.

While the operator usually does not need to know anything about preventive and corrective maintenance, the person responsible for maintenance does need to know how to operate it, at least in general terms. Thus, a great many technical manuals contain information about both operation and maintenance, and they are usually called, not unexpectedly, operation and maintenance manuals.

The manual might deal only with maintenance or only with operation, but a description of an operation and maintenance manual will cover the requirements of the more specialized manuals.

The typical operation and maintenance manual will include these basic sections:

Introduction. This section usually is quite brief, perhaps only a few pages. It will include some general statement about the purpose and scope of the manual, and it may list associated documents that are also prepared for the same equipment.

Description. This section will provide a physical description of the equipment. If appropriate, a description of electrical circuitry will be included. Depending on the size and complexity of the equipment, all descriptive material might be included in a single chapter, or the information might be divided into two or more chapters.

Operation. The description section covers the operating controls. This section provides step-by-step procedures for using them.

Maintenance. There are two kinds of maintenance: preventive and corrective. Preventive maintenance comprises everything that must be done to avoid equipment failure, including routine inspection, cleaning, and lubrication. Corrective maintenance comprises everything that must be done to get the equipment working again if a failure occurs, including troubleshooting, replacement of parts, and other repairs. Preventive and corrective maintenance are sometimes included in the same chapter; often several chapters are necessary.

Parts. The information in this section ranges from a simple list of replacement parts to an elaborate parts breakdown with exploded views of all assemblies and a detailed listing of all components, however small.

An operation and maintenance manual will, if necessary, include chapters devoted to other information, such as:

theory of operation;

special test procedures;

special tools and test equipment;

references to manufacturers' manuals from other companies, if part of the equipment is subcontracted;

drawings and diagrams listed separately, if the hardware is extensive.

The style of the technical manual is probably the most user-oriented of all technical writing. It should provide the reader all he needs to know to operate and maintain the equipment—clearly, accurately, and completely.

The division of text into sections and chapters should be designed to help the reader go directly to the information he needs. Thus, the breakdown of material into several orders of paragraph headings is standard.

The manual should be adequately illustrated, both with photographs and drawings.

All test and maintenance procedures should be provided in step-by-step fashion. The imperative voice is standard. Don't say, "The relay should be removed." Say, "Remove the relay."

The technical writer normally does not have much freedom in developing the style of a technical manual. A great many manuals are provided in fulfillment of military contracts. These contracts usually require conformance to military specifications and standards that spell out very definite rules of style and content.

Commercial manuals, which are provided with a company's own products, allow more freedom to the technical writer, but even here, most companies have strict guidelines that must be adhered to.

Figures 11-1, 11-2, and 11-3 show pages from typical operation and maintenance manuals.

PIMM-225-X

p. Secure the aft grating in position with acorn nuts (item 24 of Drawing No. E-508-H-1055). Snug the nuts until they bottom out on the bolts.

q. Remove the rigging and the 1/2-inch eyebolt from the aft grating.

NOTE

The installation of the aft switch is now complete. For connections of the hydraulic lines, refer to Drawing No. J-508-H-606. For fill and bleeding of the hydraulic system, refer to 6-49.

6-36 Removal of Midplane Trigger Switch. (See Drawing No. J-508-H-1146.) To remove the midplane trigger switch, proceed as follows:

a. Remove the switch plate as follows:

1. Place a protective split hose around the knife-edge of the switch plate (item 5) and attach the handling fixture (P/N B-508-M-913).

2. Rig the handling fixture to the A-frame hoist hook with a 1/4-inch cable.

3. Route the cable through the 1-inch hole in the intermediate coax roof (Figure 6-4).

4. Take up slack in the cable rigging.

5. Remove capscrews (item 74) that secure the switch plate to the switch assembly.

6. Remove the switch plate.

b. Remove the switch from the coax supports as follows:

1. Remove the center panels of the false ceiling.

2. Rig the support tube extension (item 10) to an overhead chain hoist and take up slack.

6-57

Figure 11-1. Page from the maintenance chapter of an operation and maintenance manual.

PIMM-180-1

2-2   MARX TANK ASSEMBLY

Each of the 12 tanks in the SIEGE II Pulse Generator is
thermally insulated for operation at outside temperatures of
-50 F to 120 F. The Marx tank assembly, whose major divisions
are the Marx generator and the oil storage compartment, includes
the following major assemblies and components:

- Capacitor stage assemblies
- Corona shields
- Marx switches
- Marx resistors
- Heaters
- Oil level indicators
- Heating, power, and oil pump controls

Figure 2-2 shows a Marx tank and a portion of the Marx
generator.

2-3   Marx Generator

The Marx generator consists of 20 stages of capacitors,
each of which has a capacitance of 1.45 μF and a working voltage of 50.5 kV. The capacitors, with associated components and
circuitry necessary for charging and firing the Marx generator,
are immersed in insulating oil, which can be pumped into the

2-4

Figure 11-2. Page from the description chapter
of an operation and maintenance manual.

FIGURE 14 Electron-beam drift chamber

22

4.3 PREPARING THE PULSERAD FOR OPERATION

NOTE: Before preparing the Pulserad for operation, the routine inspections outlined in Sections 5.2 and 5.3 should be performed.

4.3.1   Accelerator Tube Parameters

a. *Gamma Mode.* To achieve long anode life and reduce tube maintenance, it is desirable to maintain a cathode-anode spacing that minimizes anode spall. The anode material (tantalum) should be 0.030 inch thick and must be replaced whenever extreme spallation or buckling occurs. Normally, two 0.015-inch-thick layers are used. The cathode is of a 1-3/4-inch-diameter, multipoint design; the needles should be kept straight and on an even plane (within ± 1/32 inch). Cathode-anode spacing is measured from the tips of the needles to the anode surface. The cathode should be centered with respect to the anode plate. The recommended cathode-anode spacing for nominal gamma operation is 3.00 inches.

b. *Electron-Beam Mode.* In the electron-beam mode, the tantalum anode is replaced with a 0.002-inch-thick titanium or aluminized-Mylar window and the cathode-anode spacing is reduced. The recommended cathode-anode spacing for nominal electron-beam operation is determined by the electron-beam-energy level required.

In addition to the above changes, operation in the electron-beam mode requires the use of the electron-beam drift chamber. This chamber is attached to the vacuum pump-out chamber (Figure 14) and is normally operated at pressures between 0.1 and 3.0 torr. The pressure in the electron-beam chamber controls beam divergence.

Very thin anodes are used to minimize beam attenuation. The pressure in the beam chamber is controlled by a Hastings Model CVT-24 gauge, Hastings Model DV4D gauge head, a Hoke electromechanical servo leak valve, and a 17.5-cfm Welch Duo-Seal vacuum pump (see Section 4.1 for operation of these components).

Figure 11-3 (Sheet 1).   Page from an operation and maintenance manual with illustrations integrated with text.

c. *Tube Vacuum.* Tube vacuum during pulsing (gamma and electron-beam modes) should be 1×10^{-4} torr or less to increase stability and reproducibility. A significant increase in tube pressure above 1×10^{-4} torr may result in a gaseous breakdown between electrodes in the accelerator tube.

4.3.2 Marx Generator

a. Select the desired output voltage. From this voltage, determine the Marx generator charge voltage (output voltage = number of stages (23) x 1.5 x charge voltage).

b. From Figure 15, determine the required spark-gap pressure and adjust pressure accordingly.

4.3.3 Blumlein Output Switch. Determine the proper master-switch pressure from Figure 16 and adjust the switch accordingly.

4.3.4 Trigger High-Voltage Output Switch. Determine the proper trigger-switch pressure from Figure 17 and adjust the switch accordingly.

4.3.5 Oil Filling

a. Following the procedure outlined in Section 4.2, fill the Marx generator tank with insulating oil.

b. After the tank is full, wait approximately 20 minutes before firing the Pulserad. This time is necessary for the oil-filled system to rid itself of air bubbles.

This completes the initial operating preparation.

4.4 CHARGING AND FIRING IN AUTO-CHARGE MODE

4.4.1 Select Marx Generator Charge Voltage. Set the charge-voltage set-point control to the desired charging voltage.

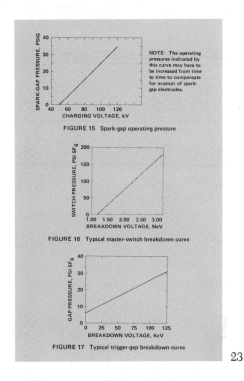

NOTE: The operating pressures indicated by this curve may have to be increased from time to time to compensate for erosion of spark-gap electrodes.

FIGURE 15 Spark-gap operating pressure

FIGURE 16 Typical master-switch breakdown curve

FIGURE 17 Typical trigger-gap breakdown curve

23

Figure 11-3 (Sheet 2). Page from an operation and maintenance manual with illustrations integrated with text.

Figure 11-1 shows a page from Section 6, the maintenance section, of an operation and maintenance manual. The page number, 6-57, is placed to the outside, as is the document number, PIMM-225-X. This is an indication that the manual is printed back to back rather than on one side only.

PIMM-225-X is a document number that tells the informed reader a number of things. Most documents published by Physics International Company start with the designation PI. The next two letters, MM, identify the document as a maintenance manual. (It is in fact an operation and maintenance manual for the Blumlein Pulser, a subsystem of a large and sophisticated system whose purpose is classified, although the operation and maintenance manuals are not.) The number 225 is part of a program designation that identifies all technical documents associated with that program. The final letter, X, means that the manual is the tenth volume in a set that actually comprises 12 volumes.

Steps p and q are the last two steps in an installation procedure.

The style of the note is one frequently encountered in technical publications, although there are other equally acceptable styles. <u>Cautions</u> and <u>warnings</u> follow the same style. A note is any explanatory material and may go either before or after the passage to which it refers. A caution draws attention to information designed to prevent damage to equipment, while a warning is designed to prevent injury or death to a person. The preferred placement of both cautions and warnings is before the passages to which they refer.

The last sentence in the note is a reference to a paragraph 6-49. The word "paragraph" in such references is usually omitted.

Paragraph 6-36 is a tertiary heading, although you would not know that from this page alone. Note the run-in text. The procedure described in this paragraph is quite involved. This technique of "steps within steps" is often used in maintenance manuals for greater clarity.

Figure 11-2 shows a page from the description section of a maintenance manual. A primary paragraph heading (2-2) and a secondary heading (2-3) occur on this page.

The listing of major assemblies and components uses bullets rather than a sequence of letters or numbers because the order of listing is not important.

The last subparagraph under 2-2 refers the reader to Figure 2-2. Since illustrations are not integrated in text in this manual, Figure 2-2 should be located on page 2-5, because of the standard rule that an illustration falls on the first page following its first reference in text.

Both the paragraph numbers and the page number indicate that this page is from Section 2 of the manual.

Both the document number and the page number are located on the left-hand side of the page. This tells you that the manual is printed back to back; that is, on both sides of each sheet. Since the page number is

2-4, an even number, you know that this is a left-hand page. If, as the editor, you had discovered the page number and document number on the right-hand side of the page, you would have recognized an error, either in typing or in the assigned page number.

Two pages from a more elaborate, and expensive, operation and maintenance manual are illustrated in Figure 11-3, Sheets 1 and 2.

Illustrations are integrated with text in an unusual way in this manual. The illustration is placed toward the outside of the page (note placement of the page number).

The manual uses a decimal system for numbering paragraph headings, combined with indentation and differences in heading styles. The book also uses a variety of type faces; note the bold face type and italics. The style of the note is different from that of Figure 11-1. And, finally, both pages and illustrations are numbered consecutively throughout the book without regard to the chapter number.

Probably the chief value of this figure is to show the varieties of style possible in a technical manual. Consistency of style, of course, should be maintained throughout.

Planning and policy manuals also vary widely, and they are often printed on standard forms developed by the company itself. Figure 11-4 illustrates a page from a planning guide, using a simple but effective company form showing the section and the subject of the page. In the reference page number PG 709.4, PG stands for the title of the manual, "Project Guidelines." The number itself tells us that we are in Section 7, subject 9, page 4.

The key to a planning and policy manual is a complete index such as that illustrated in Figure 11-5. Notice that Products A, B, and C illustrate parallel organization of coverage for similar topics. Each page in such a manual is usually dated, because these manuals are typically revised one page or section at a time, rather than all at once. Figures 11-4 and 11-5, from the same manual, were produced at different times. The paragraph numbering system illustrated allows for this kind of flexibility in revising.

Figure 11-6 shows a page from a personnel policy manual, and Figure 11-7 shows the associated "topical index" (table of contents) page. These forms show a different type of internally developed company form. They use the technique "Page 1 of 5" to ensure that no pages are missing in a section because replacement pages might be inserted improperly.

AMERICAN EXPRESS

Reference Page
PG-709.4

PROJECT GUIDELINES

Section
    Products A-Z
Subject
    Product H: Procedure Specifications

3.2 Pilot and parallel operations
    3.2.1 Plan the extent of pilot or
           parallel operations. State which
           offices are included, what data
           files are to be used, and what the
           measures are for ensuring
           accuracy. Plan to state, in
           Product J, the expected results of
           these operations. State the
           responsibilities of MIS personnel
           in the actual pilot or parallel
           operations.
    3.2.2 Describe the operating instruc-
           tions required to maintain the
           system.

4.0 Training Plan
     The training plan shows who is to be trained,
     where training is to take place, and who will
     perform the training. Plan any special
     training aids at this time. Much of this need
     is met by regular operating instructions. But
     additional aids, such as charts of transaction
     through the system, may be helpful.
     4.1 Training requirements
     4.2 Training aids

5.0 Costs
     5.1 Operating instructions for the system.
          Show costs to produce the instructions
          needed to operate the system after
          installed.
     5.2 Installation and training instructions.
          Show costs to write special instructions
          for installation and to perform training
          in system operation.

6.0 Manpower Requirements
     6.1 Responsibilities.
          State who is responsible for writing in-
          structions and performing training. Show
          each person's responsibilities for each
          task.

December 31, 1971

Figure 11-4. Page from a planning guide.
(By permission of American Express Company
and Fireman's Fund Insurance Company.)

AMERICAN EXPRESS.

PROJECT GUIDELINES

Reference Page
PG-001.3

Section
    References
Subject
    Table of Contents

PRODUCTS A-Z 700

    Introduction to Products A-Z . . . 701-1
        Introduction to Documentation . . 701-1.1
        Operations Documentation . . . 701-1.1
        Which Programs Follow A-Z . . . 701-1.1
        Growth and Storage of Documentation . 701-1.1
        Products A-Z Listed 701-1.2
        Documentation Forms 701-1.3
        Letter Attached to Products . . 701-1.3

    Explanation of Specifications . . . 701-2
        Description 701-2.1
        Procedure 701-2.1
        System Glossary 701-2.1

    Product A: Request Evaluation Report . 702-1
        Purpose of Product A 702-1.1
        Cost Under $10,000 . . . . 702-1.1
        Cost Over $10,000 . . . . 702-1.1
        Content and Format 702-1.1
        EDP Council Approval 702-1.3
        Procedure 702-1.3
        Executive Summary Report/Product A Summary 702-1.4
        Product A Response to PI&A . . 702-1.5
        Sample Product A Short Form . . 702-1.6

    Product A: Short Form 702-2
        Purpose 702-2.1
        Required Information 702-2.1
        Routing of the Request Evaluation Form 702-2.1

    Product B: Survey Plan 703
        Purpose 703.1
        Content and Format 703.1
        Appendices 703.2
        Procedure 703.2

    Product C: Result of Survey . . . 704
        Purpose 704.1
        Content and Format 704.1
        Procedure 704.2

October 30, 1972

Figure 11-5. Contents page from a planning and policy manual.
(By permission of American Express Company
and Fireman's Fund Insurance Company.)

TITLE			
COMPREHENSIVE MEDICAL			
ISSUED	PAGE		SECTION
4/1/66	1 OF 5		7-0400

D.   COMPREHENSIVE MEDICAL

The Company maintains provisions for two kinds of coverage:

- A group comprehensive medical program completely at Company expens;

-An Associated Hospital Service (Blue Cross, Blue Shield) which is available at group rates for Company staff members who wish to secure this coverage at their expense.

1.   Group Comprehensive Medical Coverage   -0401

   a.   Coverage   .10

      Regular staff members of the Company and their depend-
      ents who have been employed for three months or longer
      are eligible for coverage.

      Dependent coverage includes wife and unmarried children
      from birth to age 19.   Benefits for children do not cease
      until the policy anniversary date following their nineteenth
      birthday.   However, children may be covered to age
      twenty-three, if they are full-time students.

      Specifically excluded are temporary staff members, free
      lance staff members, consultants, and probationary staff
      members with less than three months of service with the
      Company.

   b.   Enrollment   .20

      Enrollment in the comprehensive medical insurance pro-
      gram is automatic.

      When a staff member begins work for the Company, he is
      required to complete Form GF-13a. This form provides
      all necessary enrollment information under the plan.

Figure 11-6.   Page from a personnel policy manual.

TITLE	TOPICAL INDEX INSURANCE		
ISSUED 8/1/69	PAGE 13 OF 19	SECTION	

VII. INSURANCE

    A. General Policy   7-0100

        1. Coverage   01

        2. Cost   02

        3. Responsibility   03

    B. Automobile Insurance   7-0200

        1. Coverage   01

        2. Enrollment   02

        3. Description of Benefits   03

        4. Submitting Claim Forms   04

        5. Conversion Privileges   05

        6. Reporting to the Insurance Carrier   06

    C. Business Travel   7-0300

        1. Coverage   01

        2. Enrollment   02

        3. Description of Benefits   03

        4. Submitting Claim Forms   04

        5. Conversion Privileges   05

        6. Reporting to Insurance Carrier   06

    D. Comprehensive Medical   7-0400

        1. Group Comprehensive Medical Coverage   01

        2. Associated Hospital Service - United Medical Service   02
           of New York (Blue Cross, Blue Shield)

    E. Workmen's Compensation   7-0500

        1. Coverage   01

        2. Enrollment   02

        3. Description of Benefits   03

        4. Submitting Claim Forms   04

        5. Conversion Privileges   05

        6. Reporting to Insurance Carrier   06

Figure 11-7. Topical index page.

CHAPTER TWELVE
Research Reports

The research report is essentially a document in which a scientist or engineer provides information to other scientists or engineers about the investigation of a problem. Some scientists are excellent writers who are able to reduce their findings to terms that are easily understood; many are not.

The problem of producing a well-written document is complicated by the fact that the technical editor, even when he is quite knowledgeable in the field of the reported research, is understandably reluctant to take many liberties with the original draft. The risk of distorting the meaning and compromising the accuracy of the report is great.

A research report can be quite simple and only a few pages long. Or it can be as long as, and far more complex than, a maintenance manual. A typical research report includes:

> a definition of the problem or a background discussion that presents the reasons for the research;
>
> the method of approach;
>
> a description of the research with an analysis of relevant data;
>
> the results of the investigation;
>
> conclusions and recommendations based on the research.

The style of research reports is quite variable. The writer has a great deal of freedom in deciding how he will present his information. In most companies, however, research reports are written in a style that is similar to that of other technical reports published within the company, although the language is often, of necessity, much different.

A good research report will usually have many illustrations, because tables, graphs, and photographs are essential in making the data understandable to the reader.

The first page of a relatively simple experiment report is shown in Figure 12-1. All experiment reports in the SIEGE II program were published separately from other documents and distributed within the company. Some of these reports were thought to be of interest to the customer. In these cases, they were reprinted as appendixes to progress reports. The page number, B-1, indicates that this page is the first of Appendix B. The footnote, Reference 1, cites an earlier experiment report in the same program.

The author of the report is identified in the upper right-hand corner.

The paragraph headings are very simply numbered, since these reports were usually quite short. Although the standard numbering of the first paragraph in Appendix B would be B-1, the editor felt that the routine renumbering of reports to be included in progress reports was not necessary.

Figure 12-2 illustrates a page from a more extensive research report that was prepared for presentation at the International Conference on Information Processing in Paris, June 15-20, 1959.

The document number, LMSD-48432, identifies the report as a publication of Lockheed Missiles and Space Division. The report was printed one side only; thus, the page number is centered.

Figure 12-3 illustrates a page from the conclusions and recommendations section of a research report on cold welding. As the title suggests, the conclusions and recommendations are in outline form. They are very much to the point, even terse.

The numbering system for sections and paragraphs is a good illustration of how the penchant for Roman numerals hangs on. These numerals are hard to read, and the combination of Roman and Arabic numerals looks very odd. It would be better to stick to plain Arabic numerals throughout.

Perhaps the author was determined to adhere to the old outline format which begins with I, then proceeds to A. The editor probably should have changed this to increase readability.

Figure 12-4 is a typical illustration from a research report. Photographs of traces on an oscilloscope are often provided to illustrate electrical data. The number A697 at the bottom left, is a negative number for location of the illustration if it is needed in a different publication.

Figure 12-5 is the first page of a long list of references from a different research report. There are so many variations in the style of references that it seems pointless to make any suggestions. Most companies have their own guidelines for references.

SIEGE II - Experiment Report No. 17   Paul Hersey

INTERFACE FEEDTHROUGH TESTS

1.   PURPOSE

The breakdown field strength of a simple cylinder-over-plane geometry has been established (Reference 1). Using the same experimental apparatus, further testing was designed to investigate the breakdown voltage for various types of feedthrough when the cylinder was passed through an interface of G-10 (a vacuum-impregnated epoxy-fiberglass). The following types of feedthrough were tested:

        a.   Straight through (no shaping)

        b.   Shaped

        c.   Straight through, but with plastic fillet

2.   MEASUREMENTS

The first feedthrough simply consisted of a cylinder or conductor passed through a hole in the G-10 interface. The second feedthrough had a shaped cylinder so that the hole through the interface was smaller than the cylinder (Figures 1 and 2). The third feedthrough was similar to the first, but it had a fillet of plastic around the hole (Figure 3).

_____

Reference 1:   SIEGE II - Experiment Report No. 14, "Voltage
               Breakdown of Air," originally published as Appendix
               B, PIPR-180-14, January 23, 1970.

B-1

Figure 12-1.   Page from experiment report.

LMSD-48432

MEMORY CAPACITY OF THE PLASTIC NEURON MODEL

We have already seen that the McCulloch-Pitts type of neuron model can store at most one bit per neuron, and that this can only be achieved by connecting the output back as an input. This limitation does not exist in the case of plastic models, since, by virtue of their ability to assume many different sets of s values, they can be in any one of a large number of stable configurations or states at any time.

We may define the memory capacity of a plastic neuron in the same way as we did that of the brain. For N different stable states each with a probability P_i, the memory capacity in bits will be

$$\sum_N \left(-P_i \log_2 P_i \right) \tag{1}$$

which has an upper limit

$$\log_2 N \tag{2}$$

For the plastic neuron model we have described, there are two ways to interpret what we mean by a stable state. On the one hand we may consider that two configurations are different if there is any difference in corresponding s values. On the other hand, we may take the viewpoint that two states are different only if there is some functional difference in the response which would occur to one of the possible excitations which could be applied to the neuron. This should not be confused with the macroscopic criterion which was used in defining human memory capacity.

Considering the first viewpoint, we see that the distinction between two states, which, of course, must be maintained over a long period of time for a stable memory, depends very critically upon the precision with which the s values can be

10

Figure 12-2. Page from a research report.

SECTION VII

OUTLINE OF CONCLUSIONS AND RECOMMENDATIONS

This section presents a concise outline of the conclusions,
results, and recommendations generated by Philco-Ford during
the Phase I effort on this contract.

VII.1 CONTACTOR PERFORMANCE

    A. The impulsive stress levels of all eight couples
at the measured solenoid impact velocities were
sufficiently high to induce adhesion and cold
welding.

       1. Proved experimentally for copper.

       2. Justified analytically if balls not flattened.

    B. The balls flatten during use.

       1. Proved by visual observation.

       2. Justified analytically; plastic deformation
occurs.

    C. There exists a backlash effect in the contactor
spring.

    D. Previous electrical contact data may contain system-
atic errors because some of the balls were loose in
their sockets and there was a lack of rigid mechanical and electrical contact between the copper-
beryllium spring and the main body of the contactor.

    E. The contacts are not influenced by ultraviolet
radiation.

    F. The measured values of the resistance of the contacts
are strongly dependent on temperature above 100 F.

81

Figure 12-3. Page from the conclusions and
recommendations section of a research report.

AMMRC CR 71-9

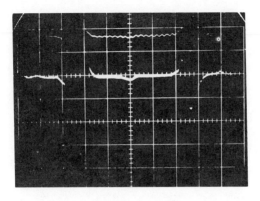

Shot 616

Sensitivity sweep:
   Lower trace: 2 V/cm
   Upper trace: 5 V/cm

Time: 0.1 μsec/cm

Figure 2.6.   Pressure response of a quartz gauge to deposition of electron
              energy in α-titanium (Shot 616)

64

A697

Figure 12-4.   Illustration page from a research report.

PIIR-14-72

REFERENCES

1. O. Buneman, Phys. Rev. 115, 503 (1959).

2. J. D. Jackson, J. Nucl. Energy, Part C, 2, 171 (1960).

3. T. E. Stringer, J. Nucl. Energy, Part C, 6, 267 (1964).

4. C. L. Hsieh and A. J. Lichtenberg, Phys. Fluids 13, 2317 (1970).

5. M. V. Babykin, P. P. Gavrin, et al., Proc. Second International Conference on Plasma Physics and Controlled Nuclear Fusion Research, Culham, 1965 (IAEA, Vienna, 1966), Vol. II, p. 851.

6. M. V. Babykin, P. P. Gavrin, et al., Sov. Phys. JETP 25, 421 (1967).

7. E. K. Zavoisky and L. I. Rudakov, Sov. Atomic Energy 23, 1171 (1967).

8. D. N. Lin and V. A. Skoryupin, Sov. Phys. JETP 26, 305 (1968).

9. A. P. Babichev, A. I. Karchevsky, et al., Sov. Phys. JETP 26, 1 (1968).

10. A. I. Karchevsky, A. P. Babichev, et al., Sov. Phys. JETP 26, 701 (1968).

11. A. I. Karchevsky, V. N. Bezmelnetsyn, et al., Sov. Phys. JETP 30, 448 (1970).

12. T. H. Jensen and F. R. Scott, Phys. Fluids 11, 1809 (1968).

23

Figure 12-5. Page from the references section
of a research report.

Figure 12-6 illustrates a different kind of format, using the traditional outline headings. (Subparagraphs in this report are numbered in parentheses.) Notice that note references are raised and enclosed in parentheses, with multiple references separated by commas. This research report was intended for internal distribution and for later journal publication.

Figure 12-7 illustrates a less technical report from a consulting firm for one of its clients. The results of the experiment would probably be more effectively presented in tabular form, with one column for the design and another for listing the average detection threshold of each. Notice that the writer chose to use indented Roman numeral headings for the major divisions of this report.

2

associated with transport functions. Freinkel et al.[15] found
that the uptake of L-alanine by rat liver slices was reduced in
the presence of 10 mM ethanol. Chambers et al.[16] demonstrated
significant inhibition of α-aminoisobutyric acid uptake by the
isolated perfused rat liver. Later, Spencer, Brody and
Lutters[17] reported that 1 M ethanol effectively depressed the
intestinal transport of L-proline and glycine. This was attri-
buted to tissue damage, rather than to a direct effect on the
transport mechanism. These observations, as well as our earlier
experience with other drugs[7,9,18], prompted us to undertake
further studies with ethanol.

The present review is divided into four parts: a) a general
consideration of active transport; b) effect of ethanol on the
intestinal absorption of amino acids in laboratory animals;
c) clinical observations; and d) a brief discussion of possible
mechanisms of action.

II. GENERAL CONSIDERATIONS

A. ACTIVE TRANSPORT

The intestinal absorption of amino acids was at first considered to be a process of passive diffusion, requiring no ex-
penditure of metabolic energy. However, most water soluble
substances (amino acids, sugars) do not penetrate the intestinal
barrier rapidly enough to supply the nutrients required for sur-
vival. The existence of an active transport mechanism was first

Figure 12-6. Research report with outline headings.

A COMPARATIVE STUDY OF HIGHWAY SIGNS

A complete description of the procedures of this study is
attached to the end of this report. Also, in the description
of the procedures is a key to the code letters assigned to the
different highway signs.

I. DETECTION THRESHOLD

Design C, a marker with the inscription "North Bay-Bridge
Tunnel" and with a pink flamingo, is the design with the best
threshold of detection. This sign can be recognized and also
read more quickly than the other designs.

The detection threshold for the signs is given below in
fractions of a second. These detection limens were determined
by means of a tachistoscopic experiment that employed 133 college students in four groups (see attached description of procedure):

     Design C -- average detection threshold 0.134 second

     Design D -- average detection threshold 0.175 second

     Design A -- average detection threshold 0.410 second

     Design B -- average detection threshold 0.600 second

     Design X -- average detection threshold 0.340 second

The difference between Design C (13/100 second) and Design
D (18/100 second) is not great, but other evidence suggests that
Design D is not as good as Design C. Highway marker signs are
complex stimuli and when separate detection thresholds are com-
puted for (a) recognition of the drawing or figure of the sign,

Figure 12-7. Research report from a consulting firm.

CHAPTER THIRTEEN
Progress Reports

Progress reports are usually issued for long-term manufacturing or research and development programs. These reports, often a contractual requirement, tell the company's management or the outside customer how a program is faring. They are published at regular intervals, which are usually established by contract.

When the program is concluded, the entire series of reports is a history of the effort on the program, but the recording of history is not the purpose of the reports. The intent of the progress report is to keep the customer informed about work on the program. Typical information sections found in progress reports are listed below.

Status of manufacturing. If the end product of the program is a system of equipment (hardware), fabrication of different portions of the system is usually going on simultaneously. This section tells exactly what fabrication has been done and indicates how nearly complete it is.

Technical and design effort. Much engineering design (and changes of design resulting from testing or problems) goes on before the design is "frozen." This section reports testing, research, and design activity.

Problems to be solved. Any large manufacturing project is likely to have problems. These must be identified to the customer and discussed. They might involve difficulties with other contractors, unforeseen obstacles in design or fabrication, or even some contractual matter that must be negotiated. It is not a good idea to burden the customer with trivialities, but it is certainly prudent to bring up problems that might be discovered later, in a more embarrassing fashion.

Financial information. The customer is certainly interested in how the money is being spent, as is the company's management. Many progress reports include a financial section that describes the funding for various parts of the program, with an indication of over- or underspending.

Figures 13-1 and 13-2 illustrate pages from two different progress reports.

Figure 13-1 seems to be part of the report on fabrication, but the parts mentioned on this page were subcontracted, so they were included under engineering design effort.

Figure 13-2 gives details about the progress of fabrication of assemblies for a large program.

Figures 13-3 and 13-4 are pages from a financial summary and status report, published as a supplement to a progress report because there are many people who are interested in the main report but would not need to see this portion.

As illustrated in Figure 13-3, the funding for the large SIEGE II program was broken down into seven categories. The bar graph for Category I is shown in Figure 13-4. The blank bars indicate projected costs, while the shaded bars show actual costs. You can see, from the location of the page number, that this was a "turn page" in the original document.

One useful technique is to include for each section of the progress report a page of "action steps," as illustrated in Figure 13-5. The use of the number symbol (#) is not standard, and in this case it is not necessary.

PIPR-180-17

SECTION IV

ENGINEERING DESIGN EFFORT

A. MARX GENERATORS

1. Marx Generator Tanks

The tenth Marx tank was delivered on February 26 and the eleventh, on March 9, 1970.

2. Marx Tank Insulation

No change in status.

3. Marx Generator Hardware

Purchase orders have been released to procure the components required for the full system.

4. Flexible Outer Conductors

The nine parts required for the full system are now being fabricated.

5. Oil/Oil Diaphragm

One diaphragm remains to be fabricated to complete the quarter-system requirements.

6. Inner Conductor

All components required for the quarter system have been received.

14

Figure 13-1. Page from the section describing the engineering design effort in a progress report.

PIPR-464-1

The program schedule, through completion of the pulse-line
checkout, is given in Figure 1.

TASK 1 - GENERATOR MODIFICATIONS

The machine modifications and assembly are proceeding
smoothly and running on or slightly ahead of schedule. Costs
are within budget. The Advanced Concepts Program (ACP) will continue testing on the OWL Facility I through the week ending on
12 January 1973. The disassembly and modifications of existing
OWL components will start the following week.

Marx Generator

Modifications to the AURORA Facility II tank are complete.
The tank was extended 8 feet and new overhead support structures
were added to allow installation of a 40-stage Marx generator.
The assembly and installation of the Marx generator, including switch gaps, gas lines, and $CuSO_4$ resistors, is complete.
High-voltage testing of the Marx generator will commence
the week of 15 January 1973.

Outer Pulse Line

The design of all outer pulse line components is complete,
and fabrication has begun.

3

Figure 13-2. Page from the section describing
the fabrication effort in a progress report.

```
                    SUPPLEMENT TO PIPR-180-17

               FINANCIAL SUMMARY AND PROGRAM STATUS

A.   INTRODUCTION

     Reprograming of SIEGE II is underway.  New cost charts, re-
flecting the revised program, will be prepared for the next progress
report.

B.   PROGRAM STATUS

     Table I presents the program status as of the end of the re-
porting period.

C.   PRIME COSTS

     Prime costs as of March 9 are shown in bar graphs for the
following categories:

                    Category 1:  System Design
                    Category 2:  Experimental Program
                    Category 3:  Quarter System
                    Category 4:  Full System
                    Category 5:  Reporting and Travel
                    Category 6:  Capacitor Tests
                    Category 7:  Total Prime Costs
```

```
                              1
```

Figure 13-3. Page from a financial summary and
description of program status in a progress report.

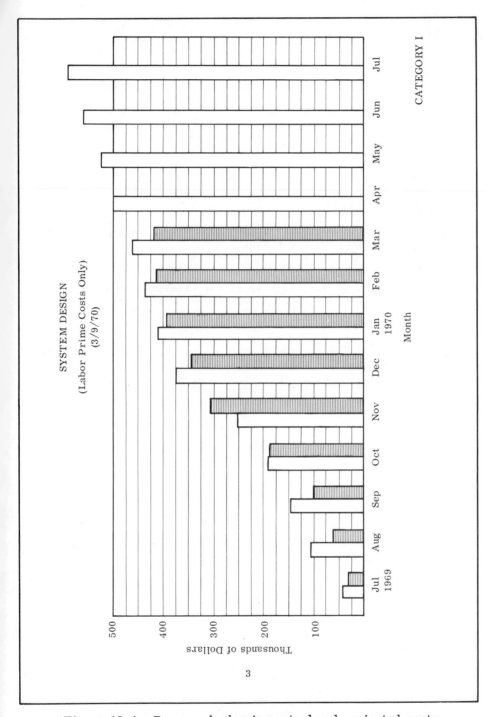

Figure 13-4. Bar graph showing actual and projected costs
in a financial supplement to a progress report.

- 17 -

ACTION STEPS #3.1.1 - 3.1.3

Action Step #3.1.1.

Train two foreign exchange traders under the guidance of Chief
Foreign Exchange Trader Johnson.

Action Step #3.1.2.

Make full and profitable use of global satellite communications
system to ensure interest and foreign exchange rates maintained competitive to attract new business and retain existing
clients.

Action Step #3.1.3.

Marketing to develop intense solicitation program on present
clients to develop additional foreign exchange business by selling competitive rates. Also marketing will utilize our foreign
exchange expertise when soliciting new clients.

Figure 13-5. "Action step" format in a progress report.

CHAPTER FOURTEEN
Brochures

Brochures are quite different from other technical documents, because they are essentially sales documents. They present, as attractively as possible, the company, its products, or its services.

Brochures are usually more expensive to publish than other technical documents. The paper is of better quality, and the printing and illustrations are usually more expensive.

While all technical writing should be of good quality, the best possible presentation is imperative in a brochure. It is the company's "foot in the door." If it does not get its message across effectively, it might not even be read.

Brochures follow many of the principles of advertising, but the selling job is still done in terms of factual information. There are, of course, brochures, in pure advertising, but the intended reader of technical brochures is not the average consumer, but a technical or professional person whose recommendations are seriously considered by management.

One characteristic of a good technical brochure, as illustrated in Figure 14-1, Sheets 1 and 2, is a clear, direct presentation of technical information about the product. In this case it is a simple data sheet, printed on both sides. The front pictures the product and gives a description of its purpose and operation. The back presents the general characteristics and price. Many brochures, of course, do not quote prices.

The inside portion of a more elaborate brochure, printed on high quality card stock, is illustrated in Figure 14-2, Sheets 1 and 2.

Some brochures are not expensive documents on high quality paper, but are designed to pack as much information as possible into a limited space. Figure 14-3 shows part of a "brochure" which is sent with prescription drug products distributed by a pharmaceutical company.

PHYSICS INTERNATIONAL
Data sheet

Number 7112

FRP-200

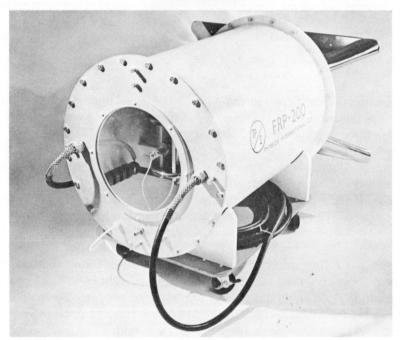

Physics International's FRP-200 is a fast-rise pulse generator designed to drive a parallel plate transmission line load. The system has three components: an adjustable ±100-kV power supply whose outputs are balanced with respect to ground, a trigger amplifier, and the pulse generator.

The pulser is contained in a cylindrical fiberglass housing 24 inches in diameter. The housing is designed to operate in an environment of sulfur hexafluoride. A gas inlet connection and a gas pressure blow-off valve are located on the metal end plate.

The ±100 kV power supply charges two capacitors which are internal to the pulse generator. Upon reaching a predetermined voltage, the spark gap in the pulser is triggered and breaks down, discharging the capacitors into the transmission line load. The magnitude of the output pulse is controlled by adjusting the gas pressure in the switch housing. Output pulse risetime and decay time are dependent upon transmission line load impedance. If impedance is approximately 100 ohms, then risetime (measured from 10 to 90 percent) is approximately 4 to 5 nsec and decay time is approximately 1 μsec. Lower impedance will generally cause an increase in risetime and a decrease in decay time.

The pulser may be operated in either balanced or unbalanced modes, i.e., transmission line plates vertical, isolated from ground, or horizontal, with one plate attached to ground. The pulser may be physically rotated 90 degrees to change modes.

Physics International Company • 2700 Merced St. San Leandro, Ca. 94577 • (415) 357-4610

Figure 14-1 (Sheet 1).   Front side of a single-page
brochure with general product description.

The general characteristics of the FRP-200 are given below:

V_{out} max, kV	200
V_{out} min, kV	33
V_{out} variability	6:1
Rated Load, R_L, Ω	100
Output Switch Gap SF_6 Pressure, psig	0–60
Mech. Adj. Spacing	No
Risetime, max (10–90%), into R_L, nsec	5
Decay Time, min (e-fold), into R_L, μsec	1
Stored Energy, max, joules	112
Externally Triggered	Optional
Price	$21,090[1]
Delivery, Days A.R.O.	90

[1]Add $5655 for optional external triggering. Jitter $\leq$ ±100 nsec.

Prices quoted are FOB San Leandro, California, and are effective
1 January 1973. All prices are subject to change without notice.

*For further information or technical assistance,
contact:* **Manager, Technical Products Division**

Physics International Company • 2700 Merced St. San Leandro, Ca. 94577 • (415) 357–4610

Figure 14-1 (Sheet 2). Back side of a single–page brochure
with description of general characteristics and price.

We have to live with our data...

At Physics International, we know the importance of accurate data. We have to live with ours.

In our field instrumentation programs, scientific data is the only product we sell. It's sometimes all we have to show for months of designing and installing instruments. If it's unreliable—or inaccurate—we wind up with substantially worse than egg on our face. So we've had to develop data acquisition systems that won't let us down.

...so do you.

But you have to live with your data, too. Especially if your job is enforcing environmental quality standards. So we developed a system that won't let you down, either.

We call it CODA.

It's a fast, accurate and versatile data acquisition system designed specifically for environmental monitoring networks. It's the best way to get real-time data from field to office. Twenty-four hours a day. Seven days a week.

Because we designed CODA to overcome the problems inherent in telemetering low level signals from environmental sensors, it has advantages you can't get in hybrid or general purpose systems.

Its greatest advantage—an exclusive* telemetering technique called frequency burst duration modulation—makes it a faster, more economical and inherently more reliable way to transmit and receive data over voice grade telephone lines and other audio communication channels.

A simple system...

CODA is a simple, compact design. It consists of two major components—a Remote Station and Control Central. The Remote Station contains circuitry for monitoring the sensors attached to it. It also contains the components for transmitting data. Up to 256 Remote Stations can be located in a monitoring network and as many as 24 sensors of any type can be attached to each station.

Control Central is usually located at the district office. It contains, among other things, address circuitry, a sequence control programmer, a data receiving network and a storage memory and data display.

*Patent pending

Figure 14-2 (Sheet 1).   Portion of a high quality brochure.

...that works like this:

In operation, the Remote Station continuously interrogates each of the sensors attached to it. At specified intervals, the programmer in Control Central sends an "address" signal to the Remote Station, requesting that station to transmit its data. The Remote Station then collects and combines the data from all of its sensors and, using the exclusive modulation technique, transmits this information as a frequency multiplexed signal to Control Central. Control Central holds this information in memory until it receives a "handshake" signal that confirms that the Remote Station is the same one that was addressed. The data is then released from memory into the display and the operation for that station is complete.

This entire process—from address signal to release from memory—takes about 0.3 second for all 24 sensors. Including the minimum time required to get the data through the telephone exchange network. On a private intra-exchange line it takes as little as 0.1 second.

...and is better because:

It's economical. For a number of reasons. First, it minimizes on-line telephone charges. If your sensors are working 24 hours a day and you transmit over a WATS line, CODA can be as much as 300 percent cheaper. That 0.3 second transmission time for all sensors makes a big difference.

In addition, CODA is a simple system compared to frequency shift keying (FSK) and other types. Its exclusive modulation technique reduces the number of expensive interface components needed to send your data and receive it accurately.

No modems. Or amplifiers. Or parity codes that take up valuable time just identifying sensors and correcting errors in transmission. And because it has no special interfaces that need calibration, it's maintenance-free for at least 6 months.

It's more accurate. Here's where CODA really shines. It's the most accurate system we know of for transmitting and receiving environmental data. Take a close look at the specs for competitive systems. They do specify accuracy—for each major component in the system. But that's not total accuracy, which includes transmission over the telephone line. We guarantee 0.5 percent accuracy with CODA—end to end.

CODA's narrow bandwidth transmission and exclusive modulation technique allow it to transmit error free in the noisiest conditions. And there aren't many things noisier than a telephone line, where spikes from switching transients alone can be as high as 10 dB. (That's three times more noise than signal.)

Imagine what that can do to your data.

Bell System statistical averages show that with conventional techniques one bit of data is in error every 1.7 seconds. If that bit just happens to be part of a sensor identity code, you won't be able to tell ozone from SO_2.

That can't happen with CODA.

Figure 14-2 (Sheet 2). Portion of a high quality brochure.

AHFS Category 8:12.16

TABLETS, U.S.P.   **FOR ORAL SOLUTION**
PENAPAR VK®
(POTASSIUM PHENOXYMETHYL PENICILLIN)

PARKE-DAVIS

DESCRIPTION

Phenoxymethyl penicillin is the phenoxymethyl analog of penicillin G.

ACTION AND PHARMACOLOGY

Phenoxymethyl penicillin exerts a bactericidal action against penicillin-sensitive microorganisms during the stage of active multiplication. It acts through the inhibition of biosynthesis of cell wall mucopeptide. It is not active against the penicillinase-producing bacteria, which include many strains of staphylococci. The drug exerts high in vitro activity against staphylococci (except penicillinase-producing strains), streptococci (groups A, C, G, H, L, and M), and pneumococci. Other organisms sensitive in vitro to phenoxymethyl penicillin are *Corynebacterium diphtheriae, Bacillus anthracis,* Clostridia, *Actinomyces bovis, Streptobacillus moniliformis, Listeria monocytogenes,* Leptospira, and *N. gonorrhoeae. Treponema pallidum* is extremely sensitive.

Phenoxymethyl penicillin has the distinct advantage over penicillin G in resistance to inactivation by gastric acid. It may be given with meals; however, blood levels are slightly higher when the drug is given on an empty stomach. Average blood levels are two to five times higher than the levels following the same dose of oral penicillin G and also show much less individual variation.

Once absorbed, phenoxymethyl penicillin is about 80% bound to serum protein. Tissue levels are highest in the kidneys, with lesser amounts in the liver, skin, and intestines. Small amounts are found in all other body tissues and the cerebrospinal fluid. The drug is excreted as rapidly as it is absorbed in individuals with normal kidney function; however, recovery of the drug from the urine indicates that only about 25% of the dose given is absorbed. In neonates, young infants, and individuals with impaired kidney function, excretion is considerably delayed.

INDICATIONS

Phenoxymethyl penicillin is indicated in the treatment of mild to moderately severe infections due to penicillin G sensitive microorganisms that are sensitive to the low serum levels common to this particular dosage form. Therapy should be guided by bacteriologic studies (including sensitivity tests) and by clinical response.

NOTE: Severe pneumonia, empyema, bacteremia, pericarditis, meningitis, and arthritis should not be treated with phenoxymethyl penicillin during the acute stage.

Indicated surgical procedures should be performed.

The following infections will usually respond to adequate dosage of phenoxymethyl penicillin:

Streptococcal infections (without bacteremia). Mild to moderate infections of the upper respiratory tract, scarlet fever, and mild erysipelas.

121 875350

NOTE: Streptococci in groups A, C, G, H, L, and M are very sensitive to penicillin. Other groups, including group D (enterococcus), are resistant.

Pneumococcal infections. Mild to moderately severe infections of the respiratory tract.

Staphylococcal infections—penicillin G sensitive. Mild infections of the skin and soft tissues.

NOTE: Reports indicate an increasing number of strains of staphylococci resistant to penicillin G, emphasizing the need for culture and sensitivity studies in treating suspected staphylococcal infections.

Fusospirochetosis (Vincent's gingivitis and pharyngitis)—Mild to moderately severe infections of the oropharynx usually respond to therapy with oral penicillin.

NOTE: Necessary dental care should be accomplished in infections involving the gum tissue.

Medical conditions in which oral penicillin therapy is indicated as prophylaxis:

For the prevention of recurrence following rheumatic fever and/or chorea: Prophylaxis with oral penicillin on a continuing basis has proven effective in preventing recurrence of these conditions.

To prevent bacterial endocarditis in patients with congenital and/or rheumatic heart lesions who are to undergo dental procedures or minor upper respiratory tract surgery or instrumentation. Prophylaxis should be instituted the day of the procedure and for two or more days following. Patients who have a past history of rheumatic fever and are receiving continuous prophylaxis may harbor increased numbers of penicillin-resistant organisms; use of another prophylactic anti-infective agent should be considered. If penicillin is to be used in these patients at surgery, the regular rheumatic fever program should be interrupted one week prior to the contemplated surgery. At the time of surgery, penicillin may be reinstituted as a prophylactic measure against the hazards of surgically induced bacteremia.

NOTE: Oral penicillin should not be used as adjunctive prophylaxis for genitourinary instrumentation or surgery, lower intestinal tract surgery, sigmoidoscopy and childbirth.

CONTRAINDICATIONS

A previous hypersensitivity reaction to any penicillin is a contraindication.

WARNING

Serious and occasionally fatal hypersensitivity (anaphylactoid) reactions have been reported in patients on penicillin therapy. Although anaphylaxis is more frequent following parenteral therapy it has occurred in patients on oral penicillins. These reactions are more apt to occur in individuals with a history of sensitivity to multiple allergens.

There have been well documented reports of individuals

LM

Figure 14-3. Pharmaceutical company brochure.

Many companies, especially larger ones, develop brochures for internal use. Figure 14-4 (Sheets 1 and 2) is from a brochure designed to introduce new project guidelines to a company's managers.

TABLE OF CONTENTS

TITLE   **PAGE**

WHAT IS THE A-Z SYSTEM? 3
WHY DO WE NEED A-Z? 3
  A Tool for Project Management 3
  A Technique for Improving the Team Interface 3
  A Method for Providing System Documentation 3

THE STRUCTURE OF A-Z 4
  Products 4
  Project Reviews 4
  Estimates 4

THE PROGRESSIVE NATURE OF A-Z 7
THE A-Z PROCESS 7
  The A-Z Products 7
  PRODUCT A—Request Evaluation 10
  PRODUCT B—Survey Plan 10
  PRODUCT C—Survey Results 11
  PRODUCT D—General Business Requirements and Design 12
  PRODUCT E—Detailed Business Requirements 12
  PRODUCT F—Detailed Design 13
  PRODUCT G—Program Specifications 13
  PRODUCT H—Procedure Specifications 14
  PRODUCT I—Developmental Test Plan 15
  PRODUCT J—System Acceptance Test Plan 16
  PRODUCT K—Programming.. 17
  PRODUCT L—Procedure Writing 18
  PRODUCT M—System Acceptance Testing 18
  PRODUCT N—System Installation 19
  PRODUCT P—Post-Evaluation 20

ILLUSTRATIONS

FIGURE   **TITLE**   **PAGE**

1   The A-Z System 5
2   Names and Categories of the A-Z Products 6
3   PI&A Request Form 8
4   Initiation of a PI&A Request 9

2

Figure 14-4 (Sheet 1). Page from brochure for internal use.
(By permission of American Express Company
and Fireman's Fund Insurance Company.)

THE A-Z SYSTEM

WHAT IS THE "A-Z SYSTEM"?

The A-Z System is simply a collection of policies, procedures, and standards developed for organizing and controlling the entire systems development process. You might say it's a "system used to develop other systems."

WHY DO WE NEED A-Z?

The A-Z System was developed for three major reasons:

    a. To help the Project Manager organize and control his project.
    b. To improve Service Organization/ User communications and teamwork.
    c. To ensure the development of adequate systems documentation.

A Tool for Project Management. The Project Manager's job of coordinating and controlling the design, development and implementation of a system is never easy. However the A-Z System by design, standardizes and regulates the system's development process, which helps considerably in simplifying the project management function.

A Technique for Improving the Service Organization/User Interface. The A-Z System encourages Service Organization and User communication and teamwork. By design, it involves the user at an early stage of system development, and keeps him involved through system implementation.

A Method for Providing System Documentation. Conscientious adherence to the A-Z System will ensure the development of complete system documentation needed for training personnel in the use of the system, for performing system maintenance, and for providing a complete historical record of the system's development.

3

Figure 14-4 (Sheet 2). Page from brochure for internal use.
(By permission of American Express Company
and Fireman's Fund Insurance Company.)

CHAPTER FIFTEEN
Specifications

The specification is one of the most demanding and important of all technical documents, because a mistake can cost your company a lot of money.

A specification is intended for procurement of hardware from a contractor and is contractually binding. It must describe—clearly, accurately, and completely—the technical requirements for items, materials, or services, including the procedures by which it will be determined that the requirements have been met.

Federal and military specifications usually have six standard sections, listed below.

Scope. This describes the coverage of the specification.

Applicable documents. All documents referenced in the specification are listed in this section.

Requirements. This section describes the specific requirements that must be met by the contractor furnishing the equipment. For example, if the item is for use in a very cold region, it must operate within a specified temperature range. If it does not, the specification is not met.

Quality assurance provisions. This section describes the tests or other procedures required to insure that the item meets all requirements of the specification.

Preparation for delivery. This section gives detailed requirements for packaging of the item for safe delivery. Usually a federal or military specification dealing with this subject is referenced.

Notes. This section is reserved for any additional remarks or explanations that may be required. Often this section has the single word of text, "None."

Figure 15-1 illustrates one page from the specification for a large system, of which the Test Cell is a part. The primary heading, "3.0 REQUIREMENTS," includes the secondary heading, "3.1 <u>Test Cell</u>," with several tertiary headings covering the specific requirements for the Test Cell. Other secondary headings will give the requirements for other parts of the system.

The block at the bottom of each page of the specification gives identifying information about the specification. The Code Identification Number 24616 is assigned to all drawings (in this company, a specification is called a drawing) associated with one contract. The drawing size, A, means that the sheet measures $8\frac{1}{2}$ by 11 inches. A B drawing would be 11 by 17 inches, and so on through much larger drawing sizes. The other numbers identify the project (508), the type of drawing (specification), and the specific drawing (1269) in the series. The revision letter, A, means that this specification has been **revised** once. If the specification is again revised, the revision letter B will be assigned. This specification is referred to as A-508-S-1269-A. The account number, 21-225, identifies the account to which work on this specification is charged. The document numbered PIMM-225-X, a page of which is shown in Figure 11-1, was charged to this same account. The illustrated page is the fifth of 12 pages.

Figure 15-2 illustrates a page from a different specification for the same system, Drawing No. A-508-S-1444-0. The suffix 0 means that the specification has not been revised. This specification, which gives certain procedural instructions, does not lend itself to the six conventional sections referred to earlier in the chapter. This page, the second and last of the specification, contains a block for approval signatures.

3.0   REQUIREMENTS

3.1   Test Cell

The subcontractor shall supply the design, equipment, and installation of the air conditioning wiring, coils, heaters, duct work, dampers, electric damper controls, temperature and humidity sensors, and electric controls, fans, chilled and hot water supply and return piping, diffusers and registers, insulation of ducts and piping, condensate drain, and appurtenances to provide a complete, operable system for the Test Cell.

3.1.1   Test Cell Temperature and Humidity

The Test Cell shall be maintained at a temperature of 74 F minimum to 76 F maximum dry-bulb temperature during steady state test conditions. Maximum relative humidity within the Test Cell shall be 55 percent. Temperature and humidity sensors shall be located in the return duct outside the Test Cell and shall be calibrated to actual Test Cell conditions.

3.1.2   Design Conditions

Summer design condition shall be ASHAE outdoor maximum; i. e., 99 F dry bulb and 84 F wet bulb.

The Test Cell is located inside the Gamma Ray Simulator Facility. Expected ambient temperature range is from 50 F to 110 F and therefore, ventilation air intake shall be 50 F to 110 F.

3.1.3   Chilled Water Supply

Chilled water at a temperature of 42 F and a total Test Cell and Data Room flow of 300 gpm is available. Maximum return temperature to the water chiller is 49 F. Location of the chilled water connections are similar to that shown on Gilboy Associates Drawing, NavFac No. 1309846. Maximum allowable subcontractor-installed chilled coil and piping head loss is 50 feet of water.

3.1.4   Heat Load

The design heat load consists of electrical equipment load within the Test Cell of 10 KW with an expected occupancy of 10 people at 290 BTU/hr sensible and 210 BTU/hr latent heat each. The Test Cell is exceedingly well insulated, so there will be negligible heat transfer through the walls.

	CODE IDENT. NO.	DWG SIZE	PROJECT NO. TYPE SERIAL NO	REV
Physics International Co. 2700 Merced St., San Leandro, Calif. 415/357-4610	24616	A	508 - S - 1269	A
	ACCOUNT NO. 21-225			SHEET 5 of 12

Figure 15-1. Page illustrating the
requirements section of a specification.

5.0 BRAZING

5.1 The brazing alloy to be used is Paste Eutec-Silweld No. 1618, which melts at 1125 F. This is a mixture of silver alloy and flux in a paste form. It should be mixed thoroughly. If paste dries out, seal lid and place jar in hot water. If then necessary, add a few drops of water and mix well. Apply with a fine artist's brush.

5.2 Brush paste generously on all surfaces to be joined: adaptor inside surfaces, tube O. D. (for about 1 inch length) and tube ends.

5.3 Position and secure the adaptor on the tube ends with the tube ends fully inserted in adaptor. Add braze material if necessary to provide ample material for the joint.

5.4 Check that items to be brazed are firmly positioned and that electrical cables are well protected from heat and spatter.

5.5. Apply torch around adaptor and heat uniformly, continuously moving around the parts to be brazed. When braze material begins to melt, move torch to apply heat directly on joint until the braze material is fully molten and flows into the voids.

5.6 Avoid unnecessary and prolonged heating after molten stage is reached.

5.7 Allow to air cool.

5.8 Remove residue flux by warm water rinse.

6.0 INSPECTION

6.1 Visually inspect joint and verify junctures are completely filled with braze material.

6.2 Pressure test the completed joint at 2000 psig with hydraulic fluid.

Approved: *S. S. Chang*
              S. S. Chang

              R. D. Ryan
              R. D. Ryan, Manager
              Mechanical Engineering Branch

	CODE IDENT. NO.	DWG SIZE	PROJECT NO ' TYPE ' SERIAL NO	REV
Physics International Co. 2700 Merced St., San Leandro, Calif. 415/357-4610	24616	A	508 - S - 1444	0
	ACCOUNT NO. 21-225		SHEET 2 of 2	

Figure 15-2. Page illustrating a
procedure section of a specification.

CHAPTER SIXTEEN

Proposals

The technical proposal is a very important document, because it is the means by which a company gets new business. The proposal may be either solicited or unsolicited.

The solicited proposal is the response of a company to a Request for Proposal (RFP), which a prospective customer, often a military agency, sends to several contractors who are considered qualified to bid on the contract.

The unsolicited proposal is also an attempt to get a new contract, but as its name implies, it originates with the company in the hope of interesting a prospective customer in a contract for goods or services.

In either case, the proposal is divided into three major sections, which may be included in a single document or, in the case of a large project, may require separate volumes. The proposal consists of:

Technical Proposal. This document (or section) is intended to convince the prospective customer that the bidder has the technical ability to do the job well. It defines the problems of development and production of the proposed equipment or system and explains how the bidder will solve them.

Management proposal. This portion of the overall proposal states how the program will be managed (a matter of great interest to the customer) and provides resumes of key personnel.

Cost proposal. This section estimates the overall costs of the program as well as the costs for specific areas of development.

The technical proposal involves efforts of people in many different positions in the company, including high management officials. It has the attention of some of the most knowledgeable people in the company because of its great importance. If you are involved in the preparation of a proposal, you will have much guidance and participation from others in your company.

Overall direction of the proposal effort rests with the publications department because of its experience with the preparation of this document and its ability to coordinate the separate (but interdependent) efforts that go on simultaneously in the preparation of the three portions of the document.

Figures 16-1 through 16-3 illustrate pages from proposals to give you a general feel for this type of document. Figure 16-1 shows a page from the technical section of a proposal; Figure 16-2 from the capabilities, or management, section; and Figure 16-3 from the cost summary.

1.3 PULSE-FORMING LINE

The pulse-forming line will be a 35-ohm, oil-dielectric
Blumlein transmission line. The diameter of the outer conductor
will be 5 feet, that of the intermediate conductor, 3.5 feet,
and that of the inner conductor, 2 feet. Although a Blumlein
of somewhat smaller dimensions would perform adequately at the
required voltages, the larger dimensions are required to accom-
modate the gas-filled output switch and the diode. The Blumlein
is illustrated in Figure 4 (Section 2).

In operation, the Marx will charge the Blumlein toward a
peak voltage of 4.0 MV in ∿1.2 μsec. The output switch will be
set to fire at 3.5 MV (∿90 percent of peak). The output pulse
thus generated, after causing the prepulse switch to break down,
will be transmitted to the diode. When the diode impedance
is adjusted to 45 Ω, the output voltage will reach a peak of
∿3.5 MV. The impedance match between the Blumlein and the
diode will result in virtually no post-pulse.

1.4 DIODE

The diode will be the standard multi-insulator design
utilizing metallic gradient rings between insulator stages.

The face plate will be hinged so that it can be rapidly
swung away to expose the insulator and cathode for servicing.

5

Figure 16-1. Page from the technical section of a proposal.

PIP-1374

Physics International Company was founded in 1962. More than one-third of its employees are degreed scientific, administrative, or managerial people, and approximately 5 percent hold Ph. D.'s. The main office, located in San Leandro, California, has 200,000 square feet of floor space. Among the special facilities offered by the Company are:

- An engine-test facility with several dynamometers and monitoring equipment

- Complete shops for machining, welding, and mechanical and electronic assembly

- A computer terminal for communication with government and industrial computer facilities

- The largest pulsed radiation service center in the world

- An in-plant explosive-testing facility and a 480-acre remote test site near Tracy, California, both equipped with ultrahigh-speed diagnostic equipment

Most of the effort on the proposed program will be performed in the Automotive Research Laboratory and the Theoretical and Computational Department.

6.1.1 <u>Automotive Research Laboratory</u>. Physics International Company has extended its automotive and internal-combustion engine research and development activities. A new building of 10,500 square feet has been procured, and engine dynamometer-testing facilities are available in three isolated test cells. Power absorption capacity is from 5 bhp at 2000 rpm to 600 bhp at

13

Figure 16-2. Page from the capabilities section of a proposal.

PIP-1217A

Physics International Company cost summary for CODA^{TM} System 112 for the State of Mississippi, Air and Water Pollution Commission, F. O. B. Location Sites at Jackson, Hernando, Biloxi, and Moss Point, Mississippi.

Control central and remote stations for operation on DDD telephone network with acoustic couplers	$14,875.00
Installation charges and an operational training program	$ 7,100.00
Option I, Printer located at control central	$ 2,010.00
Option II, Magnetic Tape Recorder located at control central	$ 9,613.00
Option III, Alarm circuits (cost per common channel at control central)	$ 411.00

Estimated costs to add monitoring stations and sensors to Physics International Company Data Transmission and Recording System Model 110A.

Item	Estimated Cost
Additional monitoring station of 5 sensors with single outputs	$3,124
Additional sensors at existing station requiring no additional equipment at central station	$ 385
Additional central station equipment for additional sensor	$ 535

10

Figure 16-3. Page from the cost section of a proposal.

CHAPTER SEVENTEEN
Abstracts

An abstract is a very short summary of a technical or scientific report. It is usually a single paragraph that briefly states the purpose of the report, the general nature of the content, and the conclusions reached.

The abstract is basically a time-saving device; it helps the reader decide whether he should read the report.

The abstract is located in the front of the report, usually just before the table of contents.

Figures 17-1 and 17-2 are examples of the abstract page. Both are from research reports.

PIIR-6-73

ABSTRACT

Physics International Company has demonstrated the concept
of an extremely low-inductance capacitor bank module using
SIEGE II 1.60-µF, 50-kV capacitors. Four such capacitors have
been connected in parallel and switched, via a triggered, gas-
dielectric rail switch, into a 9-nH, 5-megohm, resistive load.
The module operates in air at 40-kV dc (10.8 kJ stored) independ-
ently of ambient pressure and humidity. The module design is
well-suited to the parallel connection of additional capacitors
to increase the stored energy and decrease the module inductance.
The module discharge may be synchronized with a jitter of a
few nanoseconds.

ii

Figure 17-1. Abstract page from a research report.

PIIR-14-72

ABSTRACT

The electron-electron and electron-ion streaming instabilities and their nonlinear interactions are reviewed in the
context of heating dense plasma with intense relativistic
electron beams. The "hydrodynamic" instabilities (of beam,
counterstreaming plasma electronis, or plasmons) are not
considered here because the important development of the
instabilities is expected to be "kinetic" (i. e., dependent
on momentum spread). Results of recent theoretical work
are applied to plasma heating problems using parameters of
existing electron beams.

ii

Figure 17-2. Abstract page from a scientific report.

CHAPTER EIGHTEEN
Transmittal Letters

If you have a technical, professional, or management position, business letters probably account for a substantial portion of your time. If you feel the need for improvement in this area, an excellent reference is Letters that Mean Business by Gilbert, another Wiley Self-Teaching Guide.

This chapter is concerned only with transmittal letters, which accompany technical documents written and published as part of a contract.

Copies of the transmittal letter go with the document, of course, but there are also "letter only" addressees on the distribution list. These are people who need to know that the document has been published but do not need to see the document itself. Thus, such letters need to specify details such as the contract under which the document was published, the date, and the type of document.

Figures 18-1 and 18-2 illustrate two typical transmittal letters. The first letter accompanies a progress report. The second includes "letter only" addressees.

PHYSICS
INTERNATIONAL
COMPANY

20 June 1972

Director
Defense Nuclear Agency
Washington, D. C. 20305

Attention: Lt. Wm Cranston

Reference: Contract No. DNA 001-72-C-0032

Subject: "Mach Reflection Effects at High
            Overpressures"
            Bimonthly Progress Report, PIPR-376-4

Gentlemen:

    Enclosed are five copies of the bimonthly progress
report under Contract DNA 001-72-C-0032 for the period
from April 14, 1972 through June 9, 1972.

                        Respectfully,

                        M. B. Gross
                        Program Manager

                        D. W. Baum
                        Project Supervisor

MBG:dmp

2700 MERCED STREET · SAN LEANDRO, CALIFORNIA 94577 · PHONE 357-4610 (415) · TWX (910) 366-7033

Figure 18-1. Transmittal letter
accompanying a progress report.

PHYSICS
INTERNATIONAL
COMPANY

March 13, 1970

Air Force Weapons Laboratory
Attn: WLRPE, 1st Lt. H. Klaus
Kirtland Air Force Base
New Mexico 87117

Reference: Contract F29601-69-C-0150
             Progress Report No. 17 (PIPR-180-17)
             DD Form 1423, Sequence No. A002

Gentlemen:

    We submit seven copies of the seventeenth progress
report on the referenced contract.

                              Respectfully,

                              J. Bailey
                              Program Manager

                              I. Smith
                              Project Supervisor

JB:IS:crg

cc: SWMKR-2   (2)
      NDRC   (1)
      WLOP   (Letter of transmittal only)
      DCASR   (Letter of transmittal only)

2700 MERCED STREET · SAN LEANDRO, CALIFORNIA 94577 · PHONE 357-4610 (415) · TWX (910) 366-7033

Figure 18-2. Transmittal letter that
includes "letter only" addressees.

Appendix

BIBLIOGRAPHY

Bernstein, Theodore M., The Careful Writer (New York: Atheneum Publishers, 1965).

Bernstein, Theodore M., Watch Your Language (New York: Atheneum Publishers, 1958).

Comer, D. B., and Ralph R. Spillman, Modern Technical and Industrial Reports (New York: G. P. Putnam's Sons, 1962).

Dodds, Robert H., Writing for Technical and Business Magazines (New York: John Wiley & Sons, 1969).

Estrin, H. A. (ed.), Technical and Professional Writing (New York: Harcourt, Brace & World, 1955).

Fishbein, Morris, and J. F. Whelan, Medical Writing, the Technic and the Art (New York: McGraw-Hill, 1948).

Fowler, H. W., Modern English Usage, rev. ed. (London: Oxford University Press, 1965).

Gensler, Walter J., and K. D. Gensler, Writing Guide for Chemists (New York: McGraw-Hill, 1961).

Gilbert, Marilyn B., Clear Writing (New York: John Wiley & Sons, 1972).

Gilbert, Marilyn B., Letters that Mean Business (New York: John Wiley & Sons, 1973).

Gunning, Robert, Technique of Clear Writing (New York: McGraw-Hill, 1952).

Hicks, T. G., Writing for Engineering and Science (New York: McGraw-Hill, 1961).

Holscher, Harry H., How to Organize and Write a Technical Report (Patterson, New Jersey: Littlefield, Adams, 1965).

Hoover, Hardy, Essentials for the Technical Writer (New York: John Wiley & Sons, 1970).

Johnson, Thomas P., Analytical Writing, a Handbook for Business and Technical Writers (New York: Harper and Row, 1966).

Jordan, Stello (ed.), Handbook of Technical Writing Practices, Volumes 1 and 2 (New York: John Wiley & Sons, 1971).

Mandel, Siegfried, and D. L. Caldwell, Proposal and Inquiry Writing (New York: Macmillan, 1962).

Mitchell, John H., Writing for Professional and Technical Journals (New York: John Wiley & Sons, 1968).

Mitchell, John H., Handbook of Technical Communication (Belmont, California: Wadsworth Publishing Company, 1962).

Racker, Joseph, Technical Writing Techniques for Engineers (Englewood Cliffs, New Jersey: Prentice-Hall, 1960).

Rathbone, R. R., Communicating Technical Information (Reading, Massachusetts: Addison-Wesley, 1966).

Ryan, Charles W., Spelling for Adults (New York: John Wiley & Sons, 1973).

Sawyer, T. S., Specification and Engineering Writer's Manual (Chicago: Nelson Hall Company, 1960).

Strunk, William, Jr., and E. B. White, The Elements of Style (New York: Macmillan, 1959).

Tichy, H. J., Effective Writing for Engineers, Managers, Scientists (New York: John Wiley & Sons, 1966).

Trelease, Sam F., Scientific and Technical Papers (Baltimore, Maryland: Williams and Wilkins, 1958).

Turner, Rufus P., Grammar Review for Technical Writers (New York: Holt, Rinehart and Winston, 1964).

Weil, B. H. (ed.), Technical Editing (New York: Reinhold Publishing Corporation, 1958).

Weil, B. H. (ed.), The Technical Report (New York: Reinhold Publishing Corporation, 1954).

GENERAL STYLE MANUALS*

With the exception of the first two, the style manuals in this general category are listed alphabetically by author or issuing agency.

United States Government Printing Office, Style Manual, revised ed. (Washington, D.C., 1973), 548 pp. Designed for guidance in the publication of documents put out by government agencies, this style manual is extremely extensive in its coverage. In addition to containing suggestions to authors and editors, the book covers such topics as capitalization, spelling, compounding, plant names, punctuation rules, abbreviations, numerals, italics, signs and symbols, tabular work, leaderwork, footnotes, indexes and contents, datelines, addresses and signatures, the alphabets of some nineteen foreign languages, as well as information for the printing of certain government documents, such as the Congressional Record.

The University of Chicago Press, A Manual of Style, 12th ed., revised (Chicago, 1969), 546 pp. Probably the best known of all style manuals, this one has set the norm for most publications in the humanities and for most trade publishers. Its main sections include (a) planning a book; (b) rules for composition; (c) hints to authors, editors, and readers; (d) technical terms, symbols, and numerals; (e) specimens of type; and (f) indexes. The treatment of these subjects is extremely thorough.

Beckman, F., and B. Converse, Deskbook of Styles, 7th ed. (Iowa State College Press, 1944).

Chaundy, Theodore, The Printing of Mathematics (London: Oxford University Press, 1954), 105 pp.

Jordan, R. C., and M. J. Edwards, Aids to Technical Writing, Bulletin 21, University of Minnesota Engineering Experiment Station, Minneapolis, 1944, 117 pp. This useful little book covers planning for the printer; style for nonletterpress publications; preparation of manuscript for magazines; footnotes, numbers, abbreviations, symbols, equations, and tables; proofreading; photography; drawings for publication; graphical symbols; and preparation of charts and tables for lantern slides. It is generously illustrated.

---

*The lists of general style manuals, institutional style manuals, and industrial style manuals and authors' guides are provided through the courtesy of Stello Jordan, editor of Handbook of Technical Writing Practices, Volume 1. The comments are Jordan's.

Lasky, Joseph, Proofreading and Copy-Preparation (New York: Mentor Press, 1954), 656 pp. This book covers copy and proof handling in a very thorough way.

Melcher, Daniel, and Nancy Larrick, Printing and Promotion Handbook, 2nd ed. (New York: McGraw-Hill, 1956), 438 pp. Useful for information on typography, illustrations, printing processes, and materials.

Parker, William Riley, The MLA Style Sheet, revised ed. (New York: Modern Language Association, 1951), 32 pp. This reprint of an article that appeared in PMLA, Vol. 66, is a thorough treatment of the requirements of authors who submit manuscripts to the Modern Language Association. It covers preparing the manuscript, the text (textual division, subtitles, quotations, punctuation, numerals, spelling and cross-references), documentation, abbreviations, and proofreading. Some forty-six journals abide by the instructions of this style sheet.

Phillips, Arthur, Setting Mathematics: A Guide to Printers Interested in the Art (Bristol: John Wright and Sons, 1956).

Reisman, S. J. (ed.), A Style Manual for Technical Writers and Editors (New York: Macmillan, 1962), 230 pp. Reisman's book discusses the technical publications department, the types of technical publications, format, and accepted usage. It contains many illustrations. An unusual feature of the book is its $8\frac{1}{2}$ by 11-inch page size—useful in giving a visual illustration of page layout, etc.

Rose, Lisle A., Preparing Technical Material for Publication, University Engineering Experiment Station, Urbana, Illinois, 1951, 39 pp. The late Mr. Rose had abundant experience in technical writing.

Skillin, Marjorie E., Robert M. Hay, and others, Words into Type, revised ed. (New York: Appleton-Century-Crofts, 1964), 596 pp. Deals with manuscript preparation, techniques for copy preparation and proofreading, typography and illustration, style (abbreviations, numbers, punctuation, compounding), grammar, and use of words (spelling, usage, and the like).

Turner, R. P., Technical Writers and Editors Stylebook (Indianapolis: H. W. Sams, 1964), 208 pp. This style manual covers usage, spelling forms, abbreviations, punctuation, common errors, symbols, and others.

INSTITUTIONAL STYLE MANUALS

American Chemical Society, Hints to Authors (Washington, D.C., 1967), 93 pp.

American Institute of Biological Sciences, Committee on Form and Style of Conference of Biological Editors, Style Manual for Biological Journals, 2nd ed. (Washington, D.C., 1966), 117 pp. This manual covers writing, preparation of copy, approval of manuscripts and release of results, review of manuscripts, copy editing, proofing, indexing, and a list of useful references.

American Institute of Electrical Engineers, Information for Authors (New York, 1948).

American Institute of Physics, Style Manual for Guidance in the Preparation of Papers, 2nd revised ed. (New York, 1967), 42 pp. This manual was prepared for the guidance of authors submitting manuscripts to a dozen journals published by the AIP. It covers preparation of a scientific paper, general style, presentation of mathematical expressions, special characters and signs, illustrations, bibliographical references, and the history of a manuscript.

American Iron and Steel Institute, Style Manual (Norman: University of Oklahoma, 1950), 36 pp. Contains instructions to authors and covers such topics as punctuation, capitalization, tables, illustrations, abbreviations, spelling forms.

American Mathematical Society, Manual for Authors of Mathematical Papers. Reprinted from Bulletin of the American Mathematical Society, Vol. 68, No. 5, September 1962.

American Medical Association Scientific Publications Division, Style Book and Editorial Manual, 3rd ed. (Chicago: American Medical Association, 1965).

American Society of Mechanical Engineers, Style Manual for Engineering Authors and Editors (New York, 1939).

American Standards Association, Abbreviations for Scientific and Engineering Terms (Z10.1-1941) (New York, 1941). Probably the best guide in the absence of a specified authority.

American Standards Association, Abbreviations for Use on Drawings (32.13-1950) (New York, 1950).

American Standards Association, Style Manual for American Standards (PM 117) (New York, 1949).

Chemical Society (London), Handbook for Chemical Society Authors (London, 1960), 224 pp.

Dobrin, M. B., Style Guide for "Geophysics," Geophysics, Vol. 19, January 1954, pp. 141-153. Contains information on the manuscript requirements for Geophysics in regard to footnotes, headings, captions, capitalization, and abbreviations.

Fieser, Louis F., and Mary Fieser, Style Guide for Chemists (New York: Reinhold Publishing Co., 1960), 116 pp. A manual for guidance in handling chemical abbreviations, choice of terms, punctuation, etc.

Gill, Robert S., The Author-Publisher-Printer Complex, 3rd ed. (Baltimore: Williams & Wilkins, 1958). A thorough treatment of what an author needs to know if he is preparing a manuscript for book publication.

Harper and Row, Author's Manual (New York, 1966). Similar to the immediately preceding book.

John Wiley and Sons, Inc., Manuscript, 3rd ed. (New York, c. 1960).

McGraw-Hill Book Co., Inc., The McGraw-Hill Author's Book (New York, 1944), 50 pp. Another guide that fully describes an author's relations with the publisher of his book; clear and full treatment.

The New York Times Style Book for Writers and Editors (New York: McGraw-Hill, 1962).

U. S. Geological Survey, Suggestions to Authors of the Reports of the U. S. Geological Survey, 5th ed. (Washington, D.C., 1958), GPO.

INDUSTRIAL STYLE MANUALS AND AUTHORS' GUIDES

Armour Research Foundation, Instruction Manual for Preparing Research Reports, Minutes of Steering Committee Meetings, and Proposals, revised (Chicago, 1958), 45 pp, plus appendix.

Beck, L. W., and Phyllis K. Shaefer, The Preparation of Reports, 3rd ed. (Wilmington, Delaware: Hercules Powder Co., 1945), 38 pp.

Bell Telephone Laboratories, Editorial Style Guide, Editing-Production Group, Dept. 6212, 2nd ed. (Whippany, N.J., July 1967). Specifically tailored to the needs of the writer of technical and scientific presentations. Above average.

Chrysler Corp., Engineering Division, Technical Report Manual, 1955, 38 pp.

Collins Radio Co., Collins Standards for Writers and Editors, 2nd ed. (Cedar Rapids, Iowa, 1967), 214 pp. Good review of the relationship between style and thought; contains one of the most comprehensive word lists available.

Ford Motor Company, Scientific Research Staff, Standard for Scientific Research Staff Reports (Dearborn, Michigan, 1967), 76 pp.

Gaddy, L., Editorial Guide (Denver: Martin Co., 1958), approx. 206 pp. (some portions to be completed). An ambitious and useful guide.

General Motors Institute, Manual of Report Writing (General Motors Corp., 1945), 23 pp.

General Precision Systems, Inc., Proposal Style Manual, LP 7535 (Binghamton, N.Y.: General Precision Systems, Inc., Link Group, 1966), 47 pp.

General Radio Co., The Writing and Editing of Instruction Manuals, 1962, approx. 50 pp.

Holscher, H. H., How To Organize and Write a Technical Report (Toledo, Ohio: Owens-Illinois Glass Co., 1958), 54 pp. A revised version of this manual, with refreshing illustrations, is now available from a commercial publisher (Littlefield).

International Business Machines Corp., IBM Style Manual, Y20-0066-0 (White Plains, N.Y.: IBM Technical Publications Department, DPD HQ, no date), 92 pp.

Institute of Paper Chemistry, Style Manual, revised ed. (Appleton, Wisconsin, 1954), 77 pp. A compact, thorough style manual.

LeBrun, R. L., Stromberg-Carlson Style Manual, T-100, Issue 1, 1968, 27 pp.

Martin Co., Instructions for Preparing and Typing Specifications and Specification Change Notices (Denver, 1959), 24 pp.

Middleswart, F. F., Instructions for the Preparation of Engineering Department Reports, revised (Wilmington, Del.: E. I. duPont de Nemours & Co., Inc., 1953), 140 pp. Quite thorough.

Mikofsky, Bernard S., Report Writer's Manual, Bethlehem Steel Corp., Homer Research Laboratories, 1965, 77 pp.

National Aeronautics and Space Administration, NASA Publications Manual, NASA SP-7013 (Washington, D.C.: Scientific and Technical Information Division, 1964).

North American Aviation, Inc., Rocketdyne Division, Solid Rocket Division, Publication Style and Format Guide, R-1000T (McGregor, Texas, 1966), 148 pp. A careful and complete treatment of style and format for division documents.

Pauze, J. A., Style Manual for Technical Writers (Schenectady, N. Y.: Public Information Section, Research Laboratory, General Electric Co., no date), 70 pp.

Petroleum Publishing Co., Manual of Style for Editors, Compositors, and Proofreaders of the Oil and Gas Journal (Tulsa, Oklahoma, 1939), 128 pp.

Philco-Ford Corp., Technical Writing Guide (Philadelphia: Philco Technological Center, 1959), 262 pp.

Pratt & Whitney Aircraft, Technical Report Writing Procedure (East Hartford, Conn., 1955), 50 pp.

Reynolds Metal Co., Procedure Manual (Richmond Va., no date), 100 pp. The Metallurgical Research Laboratories of Reynolds also puts out a Guide for Metallurgical Research Reports (1956), 21 pp.

Schultz, Robert F., Preparing Technical Reports, Research Publication GMR-427 (Warren, Michigan: General Motors Corp., Research Laboratories, 1964), 21 pp.

Sun Oil Co., Report and Letter Writing (Philadelphia, 1955), approx. 25 pp.

Tennessee Valley Authority, Division of Chemical Engineering, Preparation of Research and Engineering Reports (Wilson Dam, Ala., 1950), 33 pp.

Tennessee Valley Authority, Engineering and Construction Department, The Preparation of Engineering Reports for the Tennessee Valley Authority, Technical Monograph 21 (Knoxville, 1942), 42 pp., plus exhibits.

Texas Instruments, Inc., Style Book (Dallas, 1960), 13 pp.

Union Carbide and Carbon Corp., Style Manual, 6th ed. (New York, 1954), 79 pp. A dictionary-style handbook, devoted chiefly to listing prescribed word forms.

U.S. Air Force, Air Research and Development Command, Preparation Of ARDC Technical Documentary Reports (Baltimore, 1957), 34 pp.

U.S. Air Force, Arnold Engineering Development Center, Report Writing Guide, revised (Tullahoma, Tenn., 1958), 56 pp.

U.S. Air Force, Guide for Preparation of Air Force Publications, AF Manual 5-1 (Washington, D.C., 1955), 171 pp., GPO.

U.S. Air Force, Wright Air Development Center, Preparation of WADC Technical Reports and WADC Technical Notes, WCOSI 56-1 (Wright-Patterson Air Force Base, Ohio, 1956), 71 pp.

U.S. Army, Style Manual, ST 32-4000 (United States Army Security Agency Training Center and School, 1966), 102 pp.

U.S. Naval Avionics Facility, <u>Preparation of Technical Publications</u>, NAFI Publication Standard No. 5 (Indianapolis, Indiana, 1960), 56 pp.

Wallace, John D., and J. B. Holding, <u>Guide to Writing and Style</u>, revised (Columbus, Ohio: Battelle Memorial Institute, 1966), 102 pp., plus appendix. This revision of the 1956 style guide by the same authors is an excellent example of the kind of help an organization can give to its technical authors; it is not only thorough but also handsomely printed.

Index

Abstracts, 239
Abbreviations, 59
Acronyms, 60
Ampersand, 65
Antecedents, 123

Books on writing, 245
Brochures, 221

Capitalization, 55
Clauses, restrictive and non-
    restrictive, 74
Colon, 80
Comma, 73
Compounding, 69
Contents, table of, 51, 201

Documents, technical, 191
Dummy, printer's, 111

Editing symbols, 130
Editing, technical, 130
Elements of style, 31

Final copy, corrections to, 138
    preparation of, 138
Format, 38
    definition of, 32
Front matter, 50, 110

Gerunds, 125
Grammar, 118
Guides, authors', 250

Halftone, 107
Headings, paragraph, 39
Hyphen, 81

Indentation, 47

Language, 55
    definition of, 32
Letters, transmittal, 242
Listings, 48

Main thought, stressing, 154
Manuals, planning or policy, 192
    style of, 247-253
    technical, 192
Map, printer's, 111
Margins, 39
Marks, proofreader's, 130
Modifiers, 147
    unit, 81

Negative, line, 106
    screened, 107
Nouns, collective, 119
Numerals, 60

Organizing the writing, 2
Outline, preparing, 6

Pages, numbering of, 47
Parallelism, 160
Phrases, cumbersome, 167
Printer's dummy, 111
Printer's package, 105
Printing, methods of, 105
Production, 96
Progress reports, 214
Pronouns, 122
Proposals, 234
Proofreader's marks, 130
Punctuation, 73
    definition of, 32

Reports, progress, 214
    research, 204
Researching the writing, 23
Review, formal, 90
    incorporation of comments, 92
    informal, 89
    technical, 88

Semicolon, 78
Sentences, functional, 143
Specifications, 230
Spelling, 69
Style, 30
    definition of, 31
    elements of, 31
    manuals, 247–253
    summary of, 34
Subject and verb, agreement of,
    118
Symbol, and, 65
    at, 65
    degree, 64
    feet, 67
    inches, 67
    minus, 66
    minutes of arc, 67
    negative, 66

(Symbol, continued)
    number, 65
    percent, 65
    plus, 66
    positive, 66
    pounds, 65
    seconds of arc, 67
Symbols, editing, 130

Technical documents, basic, 191
    editing, 130
Transmittal letters, 242

Unit modifiers, 81

Verb, agreement with subject, 118
Verbs, dilute, 177
    forceful, 176
Voice, active, 156
    imperative, 157
    passive, 156

Words and phrases, 166
Words, misuse of, 170
Writing, organization of, 2
    purpose of, 3
    researching the, 23